' I'LL BE WITH YOU IN A MINUTE, MR AMBASSADOR '

The Education of a Canadian Diplomat
in Washington

'I'll be with you in a minute, Mr Ambassador'

The Education of a Canadian Diplomat in Washington

ALLAN GOTLIEB

UNIVERSITY OF TORONTO PRESS
Toronto Buffalo London

© University of Toronto Press 1991
Toronto Buffalo London
Printed in Canada

ISBN 0-8020-5932-5 (cloth)
ISBN 0-8020-6872-3 (paper)

Printed on acid-free paper

Canadian Cataloguing in Publication Data

Gotlieb, Allan
  I'll be with you in a minute, Mr Ambassador

  (The Claude Bissell lectures, 1989–1990)
  Includes index.
  ISBN 0-8020-5932-5 (bound)   ISBN 0-8020-6872-3 (pbk.)

  1. Canada – Foreign relations – United States.
  2. Unites States – Foreign relations – Canada.
  3. Canada – Foreign relations – 1945–
  4. Gotlieb, Allan.   5. Ambassadors – Canada –
  Biography.   I. Title.   II. Series.

  FC630.G68 1991   327.71073   C91-093713-3
  F1034.G68   1991

Contents

Preface   vii

1   Traditional Diplomacy and
    the u.s. System of Government   3

2   Congress and the New Diplomacy   43

3   The Administration and
    the New Diplomacy   79

4   Beyond the New Diplomacy   117

    Index   155

To Sondra

For all that she did to advance Canada's interests during the Washington years. What we did, we did together. What I accomplished, we accomplished. Without our partnership, my story could not be told. That is because it would not have happened.

Preface

This book is about my experience in Washington while I was Canadian ambassador to the United States during the Reagan years. It is an expanded version of a course of public lectures I gave in the Faculty of Law at the University of Toronto in 1989 and 1990 while I was Claude T. Bissell Visiting Professor of Canada–United States Relations at the Centre for International Studies of that university.

One of my purposes in giving these lectures was to show how traditional diplomacy in the United States has undergone a radical transformation as a result of recent changes in the U.S. system of government. The new diplomacy, as I call it, is, to a large extent, public diplomacy and requires different skills, techniques, and attitudes than those found in traditional diplomacy, as it is practised in most countries, including Canada.

A requirement of being a successful practitioner of the new diplomacy in Washington is an understanding of how the United States governs itself. So I have tried to provide an insight into the intricacies and mysteries of the political world of Washington. This leads me to the principal theme of the lectures, which is to analyse the far-reaching implications for Canada and other countries of the changes in the U.S. system of governance that have occurred during the past decade and a half. These changes ought to be, but are not, well known to many Canadians. Indeed, they are not always understood by Americans.

It has been said that the principal challenge facing United States foreign policy since the Second World War has been how to manage its relations with the Soviet Union. For Canada, the principal challenge has been – and remains – how best to manage our relations with the United States.

The central issue comes down to this: How do we settle our differences – economic, commercial, political, environmental – with a country in which political power is so broadly diffused throughout the entire system of governance? It is to that issue, the most important one in our foreign policy, that this book is addressed. It is, in my view, the most important issue because it goes to the core of our welfare and indeed of our future as an independent country in the years ahead.

I would like to thank the Centre for International Studies at the University of Toronto for the privilege of occupying the Claude T. Bissell Visiting Professorship and for the opportunity to give the Claude Bissell Lectures. I would also like to thank the Centre for International Affairs at Harvard University, which housed and helped me while I was William Lyon Mackenzie King Visiting Professor in 1989 and began work on the themes of the lectures.

Because I am the author of the pages that follow and fill most of them with an account of my personal experience as ambassador to Washington, I tend, to confess the obvious, to write a good deal about myself. But whatever I did in Washington I did as part of a team of devoted Canadian diplomats and supporting staff that I had the honour to lead. So while the context usually requires me to write 'I,' it is often a code-word for 'we.'

I had the privilege of serving almost two full terms in Washington, more than seven years, thus making me the longest-serving Canadian ambassador in Washington since our legation was opened some sixty-five years ago. Hence I worked with many gifted officers who occupied their posts for varying lengths of time, some arriving before me and leaving soon after, some arriving recently and staying after I had gone, but most coming and going during my stay. So it is perhaps unwise of me to try to single out a few from the many dozens of devoted Canadian staff with whom I worked. Nevertheless I will do so.

Those that I would especially like to acknowledge for the role they played are a group of very gifted officers who helped guide me in my journey through the jungles of political Washington. Jonathan Fried, congressional liaison officer during the time of the free-trade negotiations, and before him, Jim Judd; the deputy chief of mission during the time of the free-trade negotiations, Leonard Legault; the two political ministers, Jeremy Kinsman during the years of the strained relationship between the Trudeau and Reagan governments, and then Paul Heinbecker in the sunnier Mulroney-Reagan years; George Rejhon and then Jim Wright, who dealt with acid rain and other environmental issues; Bill Dymond, trade expert, and Gerry Shannon and Jacques Roy, both earlier deputy chiefs of mission during my time, and Terri Colli, my executive assistant in my final years. These individuals helped me with my speeches (especially Jeremy Kinsman and Paul Heinbecker), enlightened me with their knowledge, offered me wise advice that I sometimes took, and provided me with companionship in my adventures and peregrinations.

*'I'LL BE WITH YOU IN A MINUTE,
MR AMBASSADOR'*

The Education of a Canadian Diplomat
in Washington

1

Traditional Diplomacy and the U.S. System of Government

A few days after I arrived in Washington as ambassador from my country, an American friend pointed out to me that the word 'ambassador' was mentioned several times in the United States Constitution. 'For example,' he said, 'you can sue in the Supreme Court. Our Constitution says that in all cases affecting foreign ambassadors the Supreme Court has "original jurisdiction."' 'So you see,' he stated, 'ambassadors have a certain standing in the eyes of Americans, a sort of special status. My friend, you are sanctified by our Constitution.'

Growing up in Canada, even in the rather isolated prairie town of Winnipeg, I had heard about the respect that Americans had for their Constitution and how children recited it in schools and committed parts to memory. For Canadians, allegiance to a piece of paper or even to a piece of cloth (Canadians did not possess a national flag at the time) was a difficult thing to comprehend. It was a human being, the king, who symbolized our country, our nationhood, and the British Empire.

I didn't take my friend's remarks very seriously, knowing from our Oxford days that he could be rather pedantic. But my attitude began to change when I sensed that in Washington I was indeed being treated in a somewhat different manner than I had been accustomed to back home, where I was for many years a high-ranking bureaucrat or, as the French say (it sounds even worse), 'haut fonctionnaire.' On being introduced wherever I went in Washington, I was always referred to as 'Mr Ambassador.' I began, after a while, to believe, or half-believe, that I was, perhaps, different from other people. I sensed that I was perceived as an official foreign delegate to the capital of the universe. I began actually to see myself as possessing a certain special status.

So I wasn't Mr Gotlieb, Allan, Al, or Allan Ezra, as some of my friends used to call me back home. It was 'Mr Ambassador' with the staff at the Official Residence (actually Mr Hambassador to our Spanish butler), Mr Ambassador in the White House, Mr Ambassador at the State Department, in Congress, or in restaurants or garages, and Mr Ambassador in Atlanta, St Louis, and everywhere I went across the land. This is not to say that people who called me Mr Ambassador necessarily thought that I was important. Before long I came to understand a couple of basic points about our southern neighbour: (1) in the United States only celebrities are important and (2) ambassadors are not celebrities. But being an ambassador did mean that I was treated, as was my wife, with a certain degree of deference, befitting a man whose office was mentioned several times in the most sacred American text.

Before my Washington years, which spanned almost all the decade of the eighties, I was the highest-ranking non-elected official of the Canadian foreign ministry, the 'permanent' under-secretary of state for 'external' affairs (not 'foreign' affairs because of the theory – that's all it is – that members of the British Commonwealth are not foreign to each other). As chief of the diplomatic service, I had to deal regularly with the hundred and more members of the ambassadorial core stationed in our Canadian capital, Ottawa. I always followed the Canadian custom of calling a foreign ambassador 'Your Excellency' or, for short, just plain 'Excellency.' This was really a very useful word because, if one employed it regularly, it became unnecessary to try to remember – and learn to pronounce – the foreign emissary's unpronounceable name. But 'excellency,' not being mentioned in the sacred text, has never quite made it on to the American diplomatic tongue.

It is true that some profess to detect a certain derisory, slightly mocking, quality to the term. I myself, while finding it ever so useful, could never think of the term in an entirely positive light after a very sophisticated and aristocratic ambassador to Canada whom I knew well asked me one day not to use the term in addressing him. 'It is,' he said, 'the term that a concierge in a second-class hotel in Lisbon habitually uses to greet his guests in expectation of a larger gratuity. I don't tip.'

Worse than that was a story that always stuck in my mind about a predecessor of mine in Washington long ago who insisted that his chauffeur and household staff refer to his children as 'their little excellencies.' However, I did not, during my years as under-secretary, stop using the word, finding it too much work to find a substitute. 'Mr Ambassador' was not an appropriate salutation. It is undeniably an Americanism and diplomats of the old school like myself would never use it in Canada, although 'ambassador' without the Mr was thought to be passable.

I suspect that there were some greeting me in Washington as 'Mr Ambassador' who did not necessarily employ it as a term of deference or respect. At times, I thought I detected some of that same playfulness, that tongue-in-cheek attitude, that I recall from the days when I addressed the excellencies of Ottawa. There is a most distinguished, well-bred columnist in Washington with whom I had breakfast regularly for a period of over seven years. He refused to call me by my first name (or last). I used to say to Rowland Evans, because it was he who invariably greeted me as 'Mr Ambassador,' that I could see his tongue protruding several inches into his cheek, but he was relentless and unwavering in his commitment to the title. To my entreaties of 'come off it, Rowly,' he would flash a hurt look and stick to his vocabulary.

When I arrived in Washington, I was unaccustomed to another American tradition in the use of diplomatic titles, a tradition also not followed in our country. It did not take me long to discover, in my American travels, that at almost any event or activity I was not likely to be the only Mr Ambassador present. There almost always seemed to be an American or two among my hosts or at my table or in the audience who was also Mr or Madame Ambassador. That person may have been only America's ambassador to Luxembourg or Gabon and may have served only for a term, or a year or two, and may have done so a generation or more ago. But there is rarely a foreigner who, in his travels, is not struck by how many former incumbents of that office cling to the ambassadorial title and how the community of which he or she is a part – whether it is Des Moines or Salt Lake City or Boston – courteously and graciously uses the title in addressing the former presidential appointee and seems likely to continue to do so until the end of the former envoy's days.

Whether the title confers any economic or social advantages upon the former incumbent may perhaps be debated, but there is one advantage received upon which all Americans agree: calling oneself Ambassador works wonders in making a hotel or restaurant reservation. This I can testify to from personal experience in Los Angeles, Chicago, New York, and anywhere else across the land.

Virtually all foreigners are struck by the deep fondness for titles in this, the most egalitarian of societies. De Tocqueville said of the Americans that 'it is equality for which they feel an eternal love – nothing will satisfy them without equality, and they would rather die than lose it.' Die they might, but if they don't, and manage to attend one of those typical high-powered functions in the national capital, they will most assuredly encounter a solid phalanx of Mr Secretaries, Mr Under-secretaries, Mr Ambassadors, Senators, Congressmen, and others who have not occupied the august offices concerned for many years, possibly decades. And such was my experience. Indeed, when I first arrived in Washington a lively subject of discussion was whether a certain Mr Secretary whom we would meet occasionally at dinner had served as a member of the Hoover or first Roosevelt cabinet (it was Hoover's).

It was armed with the title of Ambassador and backed by the U.S. Constitution that, in the autumn of 1981, I began my seven-year career in Washington as chief lobbyist for my country.

Did I know that this was to be my role when I took up my work in Washington? In my wildest imaginings did I think I was going to be a lobbyist, a word that for me had only the most pejorative of meanings? Absolutely not. No more absurd notion would have occurred to me.

But did I believe I was qualified for the job of ambassador in the most important capital in the world and in my country's (or any country's) diplomatic service? Did I believe I was qualified to represent Canada in the capital of the country that led the Western alliance, with which we shared responsibility for the defence of North America, with which we traded most and invested the most and shared the world's longest border and a common environment?

The answer was most assuredly yes, without any qualification. This was because I saw myself as a professional diplomat long trained in the nuances and niceties of international relations and capable of conducting diplomacy in the time-honoured discreet fashion. In the view of my colleagues in the foreign service the answer to these questions would, I believe, also have been yes and for the same good reasons. In the opinion of the media the reply, again, would have been yes because the Canadian press considered me as a friend and protégé of our then prime minster, Pierre Elliott Trudeau, who could therefore be counted on to stand up to Ronald Reagan and Uncle Sam.

In the minds of the business community I was, it is true, only an invisible bureaucrat, but businessmen were not bothered by this since the United States was their privileged market that needed no diplomatic assistance – or so they then thought. But some businessmen believed, according to our leading national magazine, that my appointment was an insult to the Americans because I was not the type who would stay up all night boozing with the rough and rowdy politicians who ran the capital and the country. This was a very strange notion to hold, given that if drunkenness ever was in style in Washington, that must have been about a century ago.

But there was one thing all these Canadians had in common. None of them thought that the prime minister of Canada was appointing someone to a job whose chief role was to be a lobbyist.

The truth of the matter is that few, if any, in Canada could judge whether I was qualified for the job or not, and this for two reasons. Few, including myself, understood the profound changes or, as the Americans like to call them, reforms, that had been taking place in the U.S. political system and in the workings of the government since the years of the Vietnam War and Watergate. The America that Canadians knew, or thought they knew, was the America they learned about in their school years or from their neighbours at their winter homes in Florida or Arizona or the America that they thought they were born to understand. Many Canadians seem to believe that physical proximity and cultural familiarity confer on them by birthright, so to speak, a special, privileged understanding of their closest neighbours and even a role of interpreter of the Americans to the rest of the world. No cherished national belief could be more divorced from the truth.

And secondly, few Canadians, including myself and my diplomatic colleagues and our media commentators, had any real knowledge of what the job of modern diplomacy in the United States is really all about.

When I look back on my term in office as ambassador for my country – the longest since our embassy opened in the 1920s – when I think about my readiness for the post, I now realize that almost everything I regarded as a qualification was, in fact, closer to being a hindrance to carrying out my tasks effectively.

My long diplomatic training prepared me for a different job in a different capital, or for Washington in a different era, but certainly not for Washington now, in the era after Vietnam and Watergate. I was still living in an age when the presidency was thought to constitute a pure concentration of almost absolute power, the era of the so-called imperial presidency, an era that ended decades ago but which many outside the United States and within believed – and may still believe – continues to this day.

I was not then aware that the tablets of political power in the United States had been brought down from the mountain, that they had been ground up into little bits and then dispersed across the political terrain of Washington, there to reside as little potent fragments of power and influence.

I was trained, like all diplomats, to deal with power that is readily identifiable, defined, and focused. I was trained in these circumstances to conduct diplomacy discreetly behind closed doors, where visibility and the limelight were to be avoided, where confidentiality was the norm, and a necessary one at that, where hierarchy and order prevailed in making rulings and decisions, where public debate and diplomacy were, so to speak, in a permanent state of natural opposition.

But not long after I arrived in the U.S. capital, I discovered that everything that I had read, studied, and mastered with regard to the art of diplomacy had to be relearned. Here traditional diplomacy, I came to understand, was a recipe for ineffectiveness, a prescription for marginality or, even worse, irrelevance. I needed to learn lesson number one of the new diplomacy: forget everything you were taught or ever knew about diplomacy.

It is a remarkable fact that diplomatic practice, as it has been generally followed through the ages and until this day, was defined only a few decades ago – in the 1950s – and enshrined by the United Nations in a universally binding treaty, an agreement to which the United States, Canada, and most other countries adhere. The Vienna Convention on Diplomatic Relations, as it is called, contains two articles that are the blackletter rules of traditional diplomatic practice; they embody hundreds of years of diplomacy. Every diplomat knows them or should; they are relevant to most of his or her activities.

The first commandment is: thou shalt conduct all official business through the intermediary of the foreign ministry. The second is even more imperious: thou shalt not intervene in the domestic affairs of the country to which thou art accredited.

In my years of diplomatic service prior to Washington I learned these rules well. As legal adviser and then deputy chief of the foreign ministry I tried dutifully, and with some success, to impose them on foreign ambassadors, especially on the American and French ambassadors, when they tried to cosy up to the powerful Canadian provinces. And judging from my experience, the rules worked well for most diplomats in most situations.

The first rule, giving primacy to the foreign ministry, was and is still not a disturbing or inhibiting feature of diplomacy in most capitals. If an ambassador has managed to establish good access to the foreign minister, or his senior deputy, or, in most instances, to the senior under-secretary responsible for his geographic area or for the subject-matter under discussion, he may consider himself, and be considered by his colleagues at his post and in his capital, to be well informed and well connected and on top of his job.

Putting aside the United States for the moment, it is a basic fact that in virtually all countries, whether democracies or not, the conduct of foreign affairs is the responsibility of the executive branch, and within that branch the foreign minister and his ministry is the true locus of authority and power. Hence an assurance, or commitment, or even a prediction about future policy that is received from that source carries considerable weight, probably a preponderant weight in the cabinet chambers of the ambassador's government, which may then consider it safe, or reasonably safe, to predicate their own actions on the ambassador's analysis or communication.

If the matter is an economic or financial one, the ambassador may in such countries establish, generally with the consent or acquiescence of the foreign ministry, direct contact with the treasury officials and, if his contacts are good, can once again consider himself to be well informed or to have communicated, with full effectiveness, his government's position on a matter. If, by supreme effort or good fortune, the diplomat develops a personal relationship with a high official in the prime minister's or cabinet office, his access will be judged exceptional.

So it is possible for a diplomat in most capitals not to feel too constrained by the channelling of official business through the foreign ministry and to believe that, if he has no more than a handful of close or intimate contacts at high levels of the key departments and offices, he will be doing his job very well indeed.

This is not to suggest that acquiring such access is easy even when limited to a small number of individuals. There is an extraordinary competition for such access in most capitals and it is a well-worn complaint – I heard it so often when I was under-secretary – that ambassadors must wait for months just to get an appointment with the top political official, if they get one at all. Domestic political pressures create time constraints that often severely limit the availability of high-ranking officials in a parliamentary system.

Nor is this to say that in all cases such access is sufficient. The foreign minister or official may not be able to provide the desired assurance for the very good reason that the foreign minister cannot commit the authority of the minister responsible for the issue – for example, if it concerns a domestic field such as transportation, or broadcasting, or immigration. Direct personal relationships with the top officials of the departments dealing with these subjects is very desirable indeed and, if achieved, reflects well on the diplomat's prowess and performance.

But, at heart, the ambassador can excel at this job with only a handful of exceptional contacts in the high regions of foreign affairs, finance, and the central cabinet office. On the basis of such privileged contacts, the ambassador can score heavily back home when, in his dispatch, he reports: 'At a tête-à-tête lunch yesterday with the deputy foreign minister, I was told in strictest confidence that his government will not object or take any action against ... or insist that we ... or expect that ... or require that ...' (or whatever, as the case may be).

Nothing is more likely to strike terror in the heart of a professional diplomat than the accusation that he is interfering in the domestic affairs of his host government. So the second black-letter injunction is well understood and faithfully followed by all good ambassadors. In fact, they live it. Occasionally an ambassador, usually an untrained, political one, may expound on the excessive nature (in his view) of the social programs of his host country or some similar domestic theme (a not unknown habit of certain appointees of President Reagan), but so great can be the sense of outrage among the local population that ambassadors are grateful for the clarity and firmness of the injunction against such comments. Even the most unimaginative of old-school diplomats will discover, however, that situations arise where the line between what is domestic and what is international is not all that clear and that these situations are increasing. To say that we live in an interdependent world is to acknowledge that one country's actions in a domestic field, whether it concerns communications, the environment, monetary or fiscal policy, or whatever, can materially affect another country's interests.

So if a diplomat wishes, or, more likely, is instructed by his principals back home, to protest a proposed domestic law or policy in his host country that could have undesirable spillover effects on his own, he may

14

find that he is perceived to be intervening in a domestic or national matter. Hence when he is instructed to address such an issue, the professional diplomat avoids embarrassment by making his protest discreetly, probably in confidence and to the executive branch alone. Most definitely, he will not want to 'go public' with his complaint. He is therefore likely to limit his approach (or démarche, in diplomatic parlance) to the executive branch of the government; that is, he will deliver a diplomatic note to the foreign ministry and will believe that he does not need to go directly to the legislative branch that is making the law.

The reason for this approach is that in most democratic societies the executive branch controls the legislative one. By restricting his conduct in this manner, the diplomat avoids the need to expose himself to public criticism, or odium, by making protests before the legislative authorities. The legislative body being an open one and most often public in its deliberations, the ambassador cannot reasonably expect to lobby legislators on a private or confidential basis.

The good diplomat will, of course, want to cultivate a few contacts among back-benchers and opposition members. They may at some future time come in handy to him – after all they may become ministers. But he will cultivate them socially, and discreetly and privately if at all possible.

The situation as it affects the practice of diplomacy in most countries can thus be summarized. The rule channelling official contacts through the foreign ministry remains intact and respected in the eyes of most diplomats and their governments. Obviously it is rather too restrictive for the active diplomat and does not provide adequate recognition of the widening range of issues and players in national capitals that can affect the interests of the diplomat's country. Hence the foreign ministry is relaxed, as a general rule, about a diplomat's contacts with such other players and acquiesces in them provided they are done discreetly, are not excessive in number, are not aimed at undermining the position on a given matter as expressed by the foreign ministry, and are conducted with the primacy of the foreign ministry in mind.

Yet even with all these qualifications, the diplomat's natural inclination, preference, and habits are to find his nest in the ample halls of the foreign ministry.

As to the second injunction, the rule prohibiting interference in the domestic affairs of the host country, it is wearing increasingly thin in contemporary international affairs as the world marches towards the global economy. But the offensive charge of interference can be dodged or its effects mitigated by discreet action linked to the executive branch only. Nevertheless, the second commandment remains a popular and holy one, although poorly adapted to the world of economic reality. The recently acquired independence of many nations makes the classic notion of sovereignty more popular than ever in most of the Third World, while in some older, industrialized states, particularly on this continent, public opinion, fanned by populist politicians, continues to view sovereignty as an unvarnished, absolute concept, as inviolable as in its nineteenth-century heyday. It is therefore seen as axiomatic that the domestic policies of a state fall within the political circumference of its sovereignty and that any attempt to 'intervene in domestic affairs' is an attempt to abridge that sovereignty.

Accordingly, the conclusion that I reached before I

16

arrived at my post in Washington was simply this: diplomacy in the traditional sense, and as defined in international treaties, maintained its tenuous hold on reality and relevance in most countries and in most circumstances. But is was under increasing strain in respect both of the proper channels and of the legitimate fields of action for diplomatic conduct.

I should have known better than to believe that these views would serve me well in the United States. After all I had studied u.s. history at the University of California at Berkeley under a great historian; I was trained as a lawyer at the Harvard Law School and, while there, studied u.s. constitutional law under a distinguished jurist; I was aware that the u.s. political system was unusually complex and I had certainly heard, and heard a great deal, about the doctrine of the separation of powers under the u.s. Constitution. Like most foreigners I also read much about the major political events in Washington in the postwar era and the great contests that had taken place between the president and the Congress, from Vietnam to Watergate. And, like most foreigners, I completely failed to understand the u.s. political system.

Again, like most foreigners, I was trained to believe in a single political concept or model that was universally applicable and of overriding significance in international relations. This single concept was, in my experience, clearly applicable to my own nation and to all others. The idea is this: every independent nation is a subject of international law that acts on the international plane, in relation to other states, through its sovereign. Be he or she called President, Prime Minister, King or Queen, Caliph, Sultan, or whatever, the sovereign has sole responsibility in the international arena for the conduct of affairs between states. It is he or she who sends his or her representative, called an ambassador, to deal with that chief executive in the other's land, or his or her delegate, that is, the foreign minister and his aides. The external personality of the state should never be confused with its internal organs. On the international plane, internal organs, such as Parliament or Congress, have no status.

There was another reason why I should have known better than to believe that this truth would serve me well in my new assignment. Direct personal experience involving an important U.S. legislator should have warned me. In the late 1970s, when Jimmy Carter and Pierre Elliott Trudeau occupied the highest offices in Washington and Ottawa, a number of long-standing and long-festering disputes affecting the boundary waters, historic treaty rights, and fishing practices of our two nations got out of hand and were referred to our highest leaders for direction. They decided that the size, number, and complexity of the issues warranted the appointment of two special ambassadors who would be instructed to try to resolve all the issues in one big negotiation. Two outstanding negotiators, wise in the political ways of their own countries, President Carter's White House counsel Lloyd Cutler and Canada's former ambassador to Washington Marcel Cadieux, were appointed and, backed by two teams, conducted negotiations for over two years. They succeeded in finding solutions to the East Coast problems; those on the West proved intractable.

A comprehensive treaty was prepared that constituted one of the most far-reaching political agreements in the history of the two countries – a blockbuster of a treaty. It turned virtually the entire Georges Bank fishery – the world's richest fishing grounds – into a resource to be jointly managed by a binational council created by the two countries. All the hotly contested species of fish that were the subject of such long dispute – cod, halibut, herring, lobster, scallops – were to be managed equitably by the joint council, which would establish quotas for the fishermen of both lands, oversee conservation measures and fishing regulations, settle cross-border disputes, and so on. Then the agreement was approved and formally signed by the high representatives of both powers, the U.S. signature being that of Secretary of State Cyrus Vance. In the United States the treaty was submitted to the Senate for approval prior to ratification, in accordance with U.S. constitutional provisions.

All in all, the arrangement represented one of the most innovative undertakings ever negotiated. And, for the United States, the arrangement in forging a huge Canadian resource into a jointly managed one, was path-breaking and historic, even to be viewed, possibly, as a step in the direction of contintentalism. The Canadian cabinet and the maritime provinces agonized, but finally approved. It wasn't ideal, the Canadians thought, but it was better than risking everything on the outcome of a boundary adjudication.

The U.S. Senate, for its part, stalled. Before long it was clear that the historic Canada–U.S. treaty would get the same treatment in the Senate as Salt II was getting, although Canada was not the USSR, was not America's enemy, and had not, according to most reports, invaded Afghanistan. The breakdown occurred because of the opposition of one member of the senatorial club, Claiborne Pell of Rhode Island, supported by

Senator Edward Kennedy of Massachusetts. The objection to the agreement was that it did not satisfy a few hundred scallop fishermen working off the coasts of Rhode Island and neighbouring Massachusetts; they were not happy with their scallop quota. What the distinguished senator from Rhode Island did was to exercise his right to senatorial courtesy; he put the treaty 'on hold.'

The State Department duly relayed the word that the treaty was stalled in the Senate. They could have advised that putting a 'hold' on the treaty was the modern equivalent of engaging in a senatorial filibuster. They used more diplomatic language to convey the news that the treaty would remain on hold forever unless Canada was prepared to reopen the document and renegotiate it, to the advantage of the senator's scallop-collecting constituents.

Canada's response was, 'No thank you.' We had negotiated the treaty with the Administration. The results embodied in the signed treaty did manage to reflect a delicate balance of interests. If we were to agree to reopen it on the U.S. side, it would most assuredly unravel on the Canadian side as well. The Canadian provinces would demand more American concessions in return for the new ones being asked of Canada. We had negotiated the treaty with the executive branch of the U.S. government, in accordance with its constitutional norms. We were not prepared to renegotiate with the distinguished senator from Rhode Island or any other senator, distinguished or otherwise. One negotiation with one government was enough.

While the treaty was lying in limbo in the U.S. Senate, Claiborne Pell attended a conference in Ottawa and fell into a contentious debate on the platform with the then deputy foreign minister, myself, on the significance of the U.S. process of ratification for the conduct of foreign affairs. 'We negotiated it once,' declared I. 'Once was enough. Foreign countries cannot be expected to engage in a two-stage negotiation: once with the president and his people, then with the Senate and theirs.' The lean, emaciated senator gave no ground. 'You should have known,' he stated, 'that the treaty would not, in its present form, have been acceptable to myself and some of my colleagues. You should have known and adjusted your negotiating stance accordingly.'

'Sir,' I asked, dumfounded, 'how were we to know? Did we not negotiate with a special envoy appointed expressly for the purpose by the president? Were we to assume that he did not work closely with the Senate? Moreover, are you and the Senate majority not of the same political party as your president? And most important of all, is your president not responsible for the conduct of your foreign affairs? We certainly thought he was, but if he didn't consult each and all of the senators, was that something that was our proper area of concern? This is a treaty negotiated and signed by the president through his delegate. Isn't that a proper and sufficient stance,' I asked, 'for a foreign government to take?'

'No,' Claiborne Pell replied. 'You should have gone directly to the Senate and the senators, and, in this instance, to the Foreign Relations Committee, and made your own political assessment. At that point, then, you should have been prepared to reopen the negotiations.' I shouted back, 'I cannot accept either of your points. We do not go behind the back of a foreign government to seek intelligence as to whether it is out of line with its own legislature and its own party. And we do not, we will not, and we cannot possibly be expected to negotiate with two organs of a foreign power, and sequentially at that.' And so the argument continued at dinner and into the night.

What the senator had to say was in every sense anathema to me. The idea of a Canadian diplomat lobbying the Congress just did not seem right. And it was certainly against the Canadian tradition. A distinguished Canadian ambassador to Washington, Arnold Heeney, had published not long before this his memoirs – *The Things That Are Caesar's* – in which he commented that the relations of an ambassador in Washington to Congress are inevitably tricky. In law they do not exist. 'Indeed,' he added, 'I recall only one occasion [in two terms in Washington] upon which I felt justified in going directly, and literally, to "the Hill."' Directly lobbying the Hill was, in his view, an impropriety. Indeed, it remained the standard practice for many years, until the mid-1970s, for the staff of the Embassy to refrain from this type of activity and, for most officers of the Embassy, Capitol Hill was off limits.

What lesson did I then learn about the country to which I was soon to be accredited? I acquired, or thought I acquired, two fundamental insights into the U.S. political system. First, that it is the lot of foreign officials, from time to time, to have to deal with some U.S. senators with wrong-headed views who are also wrong even about the proper performance of their own system, let alone the international one; and second, that the then current U.S. president was weak and ineffectual and not doing his job. A strong president, it seemed reasonable to believe, would ensure that the U.S. system worked, that his prerogatives were respected, and that the Senate did not intrude into the conduct of international negotiations. So what I thought I saw was an aberration in the U.S. system; or, more accurately, two aberrations.

When Ronald Reagan assumed office, he made Canada the destination of his first official visit outside the United States. Just two months after taking up the reins of government, he informed Prime Minister Trudeau, the Cabinet, and the assembled officials of External Affairs, of which I was one, that Carter's treaty was dead. He came to Ottawa not to praise but to bury it. In reality, the treaty had been a corpse for some time.

Nevertheless, I went back to my office in the Pearson Building quite shaken. I asked myself, How could the United States fail to see where its natural interests lie? How could it preserve, over so many decades, the goal of gaining greater influence over Canadian resources and, once achieved in so vital an area of resource management and from such a tough-minded leader as Trudeau, turn away from the goal so casually, so nonchalantly, so indifferently? Was the U.S. foreign policy becoming unhinged from its national interest? But I managed to reassure myself. 'An aberration,' I said to myself, 'it's all just an aberration. Carter didn't have the clout. The episode has no greater significance.'

Six months or so later I left my job in Ottawa to take up responsibilities in the U.S. capital. I quit Ottawa firmly believing that, in the debate with Pell, I had been absolutely right and the senator had been absolutely wrong. But there was one small problem:

whether Pell was right or wrong, the treaty was dead.

Only after wandering blindly through the thickets of Washington for many months did I begin to grasp the heraldic point: What is the use of being right about diplomatic processes and procedures if the results are wrong? The world according to Pell was, I was beginning to discover, much closer to the real world of Washington than was my own vision of it.

Many years later, and not long before I concluded my assignment in Washington, I called on Claiborne Pell to lobby him to support the Canada–U.S. Free Trade Agreement. It was a typical day for me in Washington – the sort of day I would so often pass sitting around the offices of distinguished congressmen and senators waiting to lobby them on some point and, in all probability, hearing them say to me as I entered their office and they were rushing out for a vote or to receive another supplicant – 'I'll be with you in a minute, Mr Ambassador.' Indeed, for me these words became almost a ritualistic greeting on the Hill. When I heard the predictable refrain, I could scarcely refrain from laughing. I knew that the minute was usually more like half an hour.

Still lean and emaciated, Senator Pell was now chairman of the Senate Foreign Relations Committee. I broke the ice, in accordance with the usual ritual, by chatting about the senator's own agenda. He told me of his plans to attend an international parapsychology conference in Canada that summer, the subject of psychic phenomena being close to his heart. He terminated the chit-chat with the question: 'When will the Administration be submitting the free-trade treaty to the Foreign Relations Committee for our advice and consent? And do you think it will receive the required two-thirds majority support?' 'Aha,' I replied. 'Didn't you know that this is not a treaty but an executive agreement? This agreement won't go to your committee at all but it will go to several others that must consider the complementary legislation. And not being a treaty in the formal sense used in the Constitution, but an executive agreement, it won't need the support of two-thirds of the Senate but only half. But we want your vote anyway.'

I had briefed the chairman of the Foreign Relations Committee on the constitutional niceties of the U.S. system as they applied to this agreement. I understood the system and how it worked. I had roamed the corridors of the Senate and House of Representatives for many, many months, arguing with the congressmen about the virtues of the free-trade agreement, rebutting criticism, rejecting the representations of the special-interest groups, trying to explain why the dispute-settlement provisions were constitutional and in the national interest not only of Canada but of the United States as well, and all the while endeavouring to reassure my interlocutors that this Administration had not given away the store.

As I moved from the Capitol Building to the Hart Building, to the Dirksen and the Cannon buildings, through all the miles of congressional corridors above and below ground, from the Senate Finance Committee to the Senate Energy Committee and the Judiciary Committee, to the House Ways and Means Committee and its Energy and Commerce Committee, to the offices of the whips and of the majority and minority committee leaders, to the variety of spreading subcommittees, all with or claiming forms of jurisdiction over the subject-matter of the agreement or having a role one way or another, I found often that I was carrying intelligence to the members about the position of their own government and their own colleagues. I found that I was dispelling misconceptions about the meaning of the treaty or about the legislators' own processes and laws. I sensed myself very much at home with the process, the procedures, and the players. I knew that, during my seven-year sojourn, I had come full circle, from innocent to insider, from amateur to authority, from novice to old hand. And so I knew, after the agreement was supported by the overwhelming vote of both House and Senate, that it was time for me to go home.

For someone as thoroughly immersed as I was in the practices and procedures of traditional diplomacy, I found it ironic that by the time of my departure from Washington I was coming to be regarded in the capital as a well-trained performer of the art of lobbying. Among members of the media mob, the diplomatic corps, State Department officialdom and the domestic departments, the foreign-affairs industry, members of Congress and their staff, and other adherents to the congressional culture, I was becoming a recognizable figure. As a diplomat, I was seen not as someone – to invoke the old refrain – sent abroad to lie for his country, but rather as someone sent abroad to twist arms for his country. As my time of departure grew closer, I was deluged with requests to speak, write, or pontificate on 'the Washington system' and 'what it takes to be an effective ambassador' and all that. Responding to this sizeable opportunity for self-examination, I tried to formulate a relevant description of what diplomacy was all about in the world's most important capital. I called what I was doing 'the new diplomacy,' and in my farewell speech to the National Press Club in Washington I defined the rules of this new diplomacy.

I can describe its essence in a set of uncomplicated, if unconventional, propositions. The new diplomacy consists of new rules, new nostrums to guide the diplomat in his or her perilous journey towards effectiveness in Washington. I count ten of these, and so call them a decalogue. These rules of diplomacy rest upon several main features of the U.S. system of government as it operates today, all of which affect the conduct of international affairs. These features are:

• The doctrine of the *separation of powers*. As a result of this doctrine, the Congress is a primary actor in foreign affairs and conducts activities that have a major impact on foreign interests. Indeed, Congress now micro-manages many foreign issues. For the past decade and a half or so, since the time of Watergate and Vietnam, Congress has asserted this role with increasing vigour and shows no signs of desisting from doing so. Indeed, in my time I heard more about 'the imperial Congress' than about 'the imperial Presidency.'

• The doctrine of the *sub-separation of powers*. This is a phrase I use to describe a decentralizing process that began with the breakdown of party discipline, changes to the seniority system, and other political reforms in Congress in the post-Watergate era. As a consequence, political power in the Congress has become diffused, fragmented, and atomized. There are no longer the conditions in the Senate or House of Representatives that allow the congressional leadership to achieve significant control over the members. The various so-called reforms, the decline of party discipline, and the rise of the political-action committees have accorded great independence to the individual legislators, whose activity often has transnational ramifications.

• The ability of Congress to initiate legislation. The Congress does not just 'dispose' of what the executive officers 'propose.' In effect, the legislature in Washington itself exercises true executive powers. These are principally conducted by the powerful committee and subcommittee chairmen. The United States has the only system with two executive branches, thus increasing the jeopardy of foreign interests.

• The predisposition of the Congress to use domestic laws to achieve foreign goals. Because of the dominance of the U.S. economy and the ability of powerful legislators to enact laws and regulations in favour of their domestic constituencies, foreign interests are often as affected by U.S. domestic policy as by its foreign policy. Moreover, by express design or otherwise, the extraterritorial impact of U.S. domestic legislation is a deeply entrenched feature of congressional activity.

For all these reasons the lines between what is legislative and executive and what is foreign and domestic can no longer be clearly drawn in the United States. Indeed, in light of the attacks in the Reagan years on Canada's energy and investment policies and of U.S. paralysis on environmental issues because of the opposition of special interests, it seems fair to say that at times U.S. foreign policy towards Canada might well not be foreign policy at all but simply an aggregation of domestic policy thrusts.

While the doctrine of separation of powers and checks and balances is, of course, as old as the Constitution, the same cannot be said for the phenomenon of the sub-separation of powers – a process of sub-infeudation that has led to the transfer of power in the Congress from the centre, or the party and congressional bosses, to the committee chairmen and sub-committee chairmen and to individual members of their staffs. (For example, there are now 30 committees and 97 subcommittees dealing with defence.)

Amazed at the power of individual senators and congressmen and their capacity to initiate or derail legislation, I posed a question, shortly after my arrival, to a Washington personality of unparalleled sophistication in the ways and byways of the capital. Was Congress always as it is now or had its modus operandi changed in any major way in the past decade or so? I can still recall Bob Strauss's answer: 'Gotlieb,' he said, 'the difference between Congress now and fifteen years ago is the difference between chicken-salad and chicken-shit. The words sound the same, but that's about all they do. The Congress is a completely different world from what it was fifteen years ago. If you don't understand that point, you'll understand nothing about Washington.'

This was another way of saying that the command structure of the Congress had broken down and was gone, presumably forever. Not long after receiving this, the first of many privileged tutorials from Bob Strauss, I attended a small private dinner at which Speaker Tip O'Neill reminisced on the old days. The tales he recounted about the legendary powers of Speaker Sam Rayburn, who ruled the roost from wartime days to the early sixties, seemed almost impossible to credit on the basis of the political realities of the 1980s. But although they were legendary, they were not legends. Today, the Speaker, still the most powerful person on the Hill along with the Senate majority leader, can deliver his own vote, but on most issues it is questionable whether he can deliver many others besides his own.

Having heard these tales of the power of the giants of the past, I was not astonished to read of the results that my predecessor Arnold Heeney achieved during his one visit to the Hill a couple of decades before my time. He described them thus: 'I had learned one morning of the imminent threat that one of the recurrent bills to authorize further diversion of Great Lakes water at Chicago would be adopted by the Senate within a matter of hours. This was something that Canada, with the support of the State Department had resisted successfully over the years. What to do? The State Department had done its best but was impotent. I drove post-haste to the Hill. Once there, a couple of discreet telephone calls from a friendly senator brought me quickly into the presence of the majority leader. I explained the basis of Canadian opposition to further diversion ... and within minutes the crisis was avoided. The bill, he assured me, would not pass. The majority leader was Lyndon B. Johnson.'

Such powers cannot be found in anybody's hands in Washington today, whether those of the Speaker or the President.

There is one overriding consequence for diplomacy: a foreign ambassador to Washington is accredited neither to a government nor even to a system. He is accredited to an unstable mass of people, forces, and interests that are constantly shifting, aligning, and realigning in ways that can affect or damage the interests of the country he represents. So complex is this mass, so unstable its properties, so shifting the terrain on which it rests that the only way to describe the phenomenon is by recourse to metaphors, and mixed ones at that.

I see the Washington political scene as a mass or physical field or continuum in which myriad electrons or particles are constantly moving about, as in an atom, in seemingly infinite patterns and designs. Each particle is charged with power. Some of the elements have more power than others but all have power of some kind. The particle that is the president is charged, as a rule, with more power than most other particles, but the power emitted by that particle is not constant, and, in some patterns or formations, other particles may emit charges that are equally or more potent. The Speaker of the House, the majority and minority leaders in both houses, the whips, and the chairmen of committees and of the proliferating subcommittees may all be charged with very specific power, exceeding, at times, the power of the president and the cabinet secretaries and other topranking officials, all of which in turn emit charges of greatly varying strength. Indeed, the particle that is one senator may be sufficient to neutralize or put 'on hold' the movements of all the others. Some of the particles are barons of the media, some are celebrity columnists, some are permanent members of the foreign-policy industry, others are congressional staffers, some are lobbyists registered and unregistered, some are lawyers, some are former

31

secretaries, some are future ones, some are hostesses, and many fall into no particular category at all. Just how complex are the centres of power almost defies description.

Included in what I call 'the Third House of Congress' are:

- The 54,750 lawyers at the D.C. Bar, almost all interested or involved in government. (In 1980 there were 'only' 33,000 or so, but that was before deregulation!)
- Some 3,200 lobbying trade associations in the Washington area. The total lobbying population of this group is estimated at approximately 80,000-plus. Some groups such as the National Rifle Association or the American Medical Association have many more employees than others, but the average number per congressman is over 165.
- Registered and unregistered lobbyists in the many thousands. In 1990 there were, according to the clerk of the House of Representatives, 10,926 'client registrants' who filed under the Federal Regulation of Lobbying Act, including over 5,200 registrants who were not themselves principals of any enterprise. Beyond that, some 23,200 registrants had not refiled within the previous two years. All these figures probably grossly underestimate the numbers of persons lobbying on the Hill.
- Some 786 active registrants under the 'Foreign Agents Registration Act,' comprising 3,574 filing individuals, according to the latest statistics available to me (for 1986).
- Some 4,647 correspondents, editors, and reporters, according to National Press Club estimates.

- Some 4,172 political-action committees (PACs), as of mid-1988.
- An estimated 75 'think-tanks' established in greater Washington.
- Public-affairs and other types of consultants numbering in the thousands.

Supporting the 535 members of Congress are some 19,000 staffers on the Hill (about 11,700 in the House and over 7,100 in the Senate). Add to this the federal public service, which as of 1988 comprised some 358,402 federal civilian civil servants in the Washington metropolitan area.

All this makes up a political community in Washington of perhaps half a million individuals or more working in, around, for and against, or on the margins of the U.S. political system. That is the governmental community in which 150 or so embassies, the largest diplomatic corps in the world, ply their trade.

The task of the diplomat is to learn the identity of these particles, study their behavioural patterns, gain access to their immediate field of activity, and try to neutralize them or prevent them from aligning in ways that can injure or damage the interests he has been mandated to protect.

Thus, in order to succeed, or to have even a chance of succeeding, the diplomat has to enter into the physical field; he has to become a particle, so to speak, and be able to carry a charge of his own, no matter how modest, so that he can, in some manner, refract or repel the power of the others. The particles are the players in the political contests of Washington, the participants in the vast number of decisions that are embodied in the laws, regulations, directives, guidelines, processes, and other outcomes that emanate from the various centres of power on any ordinary day in the nation's capital.

If this is an accurate description of the political environment in which a foreign ambassador or other embassy official must operate in Washington, it follows that there are certain guides to action that he or she must follow.

The first requirement is for the diplomat to recognize that the particular process by which a decision is reached in Washington is often so complex and mysterious that it defies comprehension. One must do one's best to understand the activity concerned, but as Sir Nicholas Henderson, the gifted British ambassador to the United States who represented his country when I arrived in Washington, related to me on my first courtesy call in the capital: 'Gotlieb, anyone who tells you that he understands how a particular decision was made in Washington is either a fool or a liar.'

This point notwithstanding, the most important requirement for effective diplomacy in Washington is the ability to gain access to the participants in the decision-making process. A diplomat needs access, more access, and ever more access. The greater the number of players in the political arena, the greater the scope of the access required. No ingredient in the recipe for effectiveness surpasses access in its value. Without access, the diplomat is a dud. This is the second rule to remember. But it is also necessary to remember that the mere fact of being an ambassador in no way assures access.

Third, given the vast number of players in the field of decision making, and the great difficulty of predicting their likely behaviour, the highest possible premium must be placed on political intelligence. This intelligence must extend to the motives, thinking, and strategies of those engaged in the processes of making decisions. To this end, it is profoundly important to grasp one point in particular: in Washington, gossip is intelligence.

Fourth, since there are so many participants in decision making, so many special-interest and pressure groups and so many shifting alliances, a diplomat cannot design any grand or overarching strategy to further his nation's interests. He must grasp the fact that every issue involves its own microstrategy and that every microstrategy is unique. There must be an analysis of each individual politician, each special interest, each potential intervenor, and every force and point of pressure involved in the matter at hand. Each and every congressional subcommittee involved in an issue requires the most meticulous microanalysis, with separate substrategies defined for influencing the attitude of each legislator as well as his or her congressional staffers. John Brademas, a long-serving and astute former congressman once explained: 'A chairman of a congressional committee or subcommittee who knows what he is doing and is persistent enough can write the law of the land.'

Fifth, in addressing the influence of hostile special interests, an ambassador must recognize that in Washington a foreign power is itself just another special interest and not a very special one at that. And his country is disadvantaged at least in one respect: it sends no congressmen or senators to Washington.

It follows, sixth, that as a general rule a foreign power has no permanent friends or adversaries in Washington. A congressional ally on one issue of concern to the foreign country is easily a congressional enemy on another. Hence the ambassador is always seeking allies in the u.s. domestic arena with whose interests he can align on the particular issue at hand. Senator Patrick Daniel Moynihan of New York, who was a splendid ally of Canada on the issues of acid-rain controls and free trade, was a formidable adversary in our border-broadcasting dispute and a strong complainant about the export of certain fruits from the Maritimes.

Note that I say that, *as a general rule*, foreign powers have no permanent friends in the political world of Washington. There are, perhaps, exceptions that arise from time to time. Occasionally a senator or congressman goes out of his or her way to try to learn about the problems and point of view of a friendly country and so can be depended upon to lend a sympathetic ear. So far as Canada was concerned, this was true both of Patrick Daniel Moynihan, Democratic senator from New York, and of John Chafee, the Republican senator from Rhode Island; they could always be counted on to make a special effort to understand the Canadian view on a point at issue. But this is a very different thing from saying that a friend in court, so to speak, would intervene on your behalf if his constituents' interests went the other way.

Seventh, it is equally true that a foreign government has no permanent friends even within the Administration. Power within the Administration, in some ways, like power within the Congress, tends to be dispersed and fragmented, so the ambassador must pursue alliances and coalitions among the various actors within the executive branch itself. On the matter of electricity imports, the Secretary of Energy may be your ally, but on acid-rain controls he may be your enemy. Or vice versa.

Eighth, no permanent solutions are within the reach of the ambassador or his government, only temporary ones. Instability is the norm, alliances and coalitions are always being forged, forces and counterforces are always mounting. To apply a precept of Yogi Berra, in the U.S. Congress it's never over until it's over and it's never over. Canada won in its dispute about asbestos with the U.S. regulatory authorities. Canada won in a dispute over subsidies for processed pork. Then it lost on asbestos and it lost in the pork countervail dispute. The same has been true in the conflict over subsidies in respect of softwood lumber. In 1983, Canada was the victor in the softwood-lumber case, the biggest fight over countervailing duties in our joint history. Three years later, on the same facts, we lost on a key preliminary ruling and had no choice but to settle.

Because of the competition for access and influence, publicity helps to bring attention to the ambassador's cause. He must seek publicity because publicity helps to achieve effectiveness. So the ninth rule is, in Washington, effective diplomacy usually means public diplomacy. But it must be practised with considerable finesse. If you speak out publicly on acid rain, you may be accused of interfering in U.S. domestic affairs. But if you don't speak out publicly on acid rain, you probably won't get your message across. If you are doing it only privately with key legislators, the media will say you're not doing it at all and so your credibility could be undermined back home.

But in Washington, every country is famous for

only fifteen minutes. The United States itself chooses the fifteen minutes. Its domestic agenda usually dominates the scene.

Finally – but not least important – the ambassador must recognize that the best and often the only way to gain access to all the key players is through the social route. In Washington, parties are a continuation of work by other means.

This is why Washington is known for its hostesses. When I arrived in Washington, access to the White House was very difficult for me to achieve because relations between the Reagan administration and the government of Pierre Elliott Trudeau, which I represented, were not warm. In fact, tensions over our national energy and investment policies were at a high point – the strains at the top level not having been so high since the days of John Diefenbaker and John Kennedy. The personal relationships that my wife managed to establish with the wives of some of Reagan's closest aides led to their husbands accepting invitations to our embassy. In turn, this led to easy and eventually – as it seemed to others – privileged access to the White House and the Cabinet. So if I had any success in Washington, the social route paved the way. To be 'the hottest embassy in Washington' was my chief diplomatic asset in a town where most diplomats are permanently marginalized.

To follow these ten propositions assiduously is a daunting task for a diplomat. One may pursue them with considerable distinction and yet not get very far in protecting one's country's interests. Two conclusions are, however, reasonably certain. One is that if the ambassador does not conduct himself in accordance with these guidelines, he or she will likely not accomplish very much. The other is best conveyed by a comment of a wise predecessor of mine in Washington, the same Marcel Cadieux who negotiated the aborted East Coast fisheries agreement. When asked whether there was anything that could be done which would indeed improve the relationship of Canada and the United States, he replied, 'It's quite simple. All you have to do is change the American Constitution.'

The notion, as Marcel Cadieux was well aware, is absurd. One can have complete confidence that the u.s. Constitution will not, in any significant way, be changed. The United States recently completed a year-long celebration of the bicentenary of its Constitution. And yet, during all the extended parade of events, of signings and stagings and colloquia and conferences, debates, receptions, dinners, pageants and historical re-enactments – all conducted, one must note, with rather large doses of self-congratulation – almost no serious consideration was given, in any political forum or context, to reform of that country's written constitution. Some distinguished former senior officials – constitutional experts – such as Lloyd Cutler, tried to influence events in this direction but met with scant success. The diplomat must accept the political context, as designed in the Constitution, as firm and immutable.

But the foreign envoy would make a drastic error if he or she believed that the *un*written constitution should be seen in a similar way. In fact, the processes and procedures in Washington – the rules of the game – change so rapidly that even the politicians cannot keep up.

Sometimes the Congress changes the rules itself, as it did some fifteen years ago in altering the congressional seniority system or the regulations governing campaign financing, or when it established independent prosecutors, or when it allowed subcommittees to proliferate. Sometimes the judiciary changes the basic rules of governing, as when it prohibited the delegation of congressional authority in a manner that encroaches on the executive veto power.

And sometimes the media changes the unwritten rules more decisively than anyone else – for example, concerning sexual indiscretion as a disqualifier in the holding of public office (for President Kennedy it was not; for presidential candidate Gary Hart it was) or drunkenness, alleged or otherwise (as in the unprecedented rejection of President Bush's nominee, Senator John Tower, for secretary of defence). Indeed, there are knowledgeable Washingtonians who believe that, given that the rules of U.S. politics can change almost overnight, the worst mistake a politician can make is to look at the political practices of today and think they will apply tomorrow. The powerful Speaker of the House of Representatives, Jim Wright, and more than a few senators (graced with the title 'the Keating Five'), were caught up in one of these historic shifts in the rules of acceptable congressional behaviour brought about by the savings-and-loan crisis. What was once mere 'constituency work' came increasingly to be seen as gross unethical behaviour.

For all these reasons, the foreign diplomat should expect to carry on his or her work in a constitutional context that, while formally immutable, is in fact transforming itself into new ways of doing things all the time and usually changing in the direction of ever-greater specificity and complexity. The key advice for the outsider to follow is this: in U.S. domestic affairs, what is done today is not a reliable guide for what can be done tomorrow.

The basic element of political life, then, is the impermanence of the current rules. Of equal significance is the prevailing opinion in the capital that all rule changes are 'reforms' and must be seen as good. And of ever greater significance is the reality that whatever the rules may be, there are no referees – other than, of course, the media.

In the pages that follow, I will endeavour to describe what it is like for a foreign envoy to cope with his country's problems within the various circles of power that exist in the political galaxy of Washington.

2

Congress and the New Diplomacy

Having discussed, in a preliminary way, the structure of political power in Washington, I will now try to describe the peculiar features of the position of a foreign embassy in Washington in dealing with the American political process.

To recapitulate, the platform from which a foreign embassy must survey the political field and launch its activities rests on four great pillars:

• The unique American doctrine of checks and balances, the separation of powers, whereby Congress enjoys substantial power in foreign affairs.
• The new doctrine of the sub-separation of powers within the Congress, by which political power has become subinfeudated, atomized, and dispersed among hundreds of players.
• The reality that, in Washington, dominated as it is by special interests, a foreign power is just another special interest, and not a very special one at that.
• The fact that the basic principle of international law that all official business must be transacted

43

through the executive branch of the government is no longer an acceptable basis for the conduct of diplomacy in Washington.

The implications for diplomacy of these phenomena are far-reaching.

As for the first, the separation of powers, the implications are especially significant when one considers that the Congress initiates legislation and thus, in effect, exercises true executive power. The Congress proposes, the Congress disposes. This is true more than ever before.

The implications of the second point are equally far-reaching in that each congressional committee or subcommittee chairman and his staff become the strategic centre for planning and adopting legislation. That is to say, they become the focal point for the lobbying process. The fragmentation of power inevitably places high value on the ability to get access to the players upon whom power has devolved.

And because a foreign power is just another special interest in Washington, domestic interests are greatly advantaged over foreign ones in the trade and economic areas, where Congress has paramount powers.

As to the limited power and influence of the executive branch and especially of the foreign ministry in the policy process, a whole new style of diplomacy is ordained for those whose task it is to promote and protect their country's well-being in the United States.

To be an effective ambassador in the United States it is necessary to rip up the old rules of diplomacy and follow new ones which, however, are ill-defined, unchartered, treacherous, and capable of leading the foreign representative into troubled waters.

When I was still under-secretary of state for external affairs, the East Coast fisheries fiasco had helped prepare me, in some degree, for dealing with the U.S. governmental process. If the United States could, thanks to two senators, walk away from the most far-reaching resource treaty ever negotiated between our two countries – creating a long-term joint-management scheme covering over twenty-eight species (virtually the whole of the fish stock in the richest fishing grounds in the world) – well, Canada had better respect the powers of the Senate in the foreign-policy process. I emphasize the words *foreign policy* because the treaty addressed serious bilateral disputes of long standing. It was negotiated by two special envoys appointed by the president and prime minister. It covered the territorial sea and 200-mile fishing zones of two countries, it created a remarkable new international structure, and was considered in the Senate's Foreign Relations Committee.

It was not, however, until I got into my ambassadorial harness that I grasped the larger significance of the congressional role. That did not take long. Within a few months of my arrival in late 1981 – just as a severe economic recession took hold in both countries – I found myself dealing with a large number of serious threats to Canadian interests. Most of those threats arose not as a result of U.S. foreign policy or any congressional attempt to legislate in any field that would normally be regarded as within the purview of classic international relations or foreign policy. Nor could they even be described as trade issues – certainly not of the traditional type.

Disputes between nations normally arise through conflicts of public policies espoused by two or more sovereign governments. In the case of Canada and the United States, there have been many examples, over the years, when one government adopts policies which threaten the other's interests or create in the other party an apprehension of its interests being harmed. Yet, all in all, considering the extent of the relationship, such incidents have not been that numerous.

For the United States, public policies may lie in a variety of fields:

- In the territorial, navigational, or military field, as for example, when the United States in 1969 directly challenged our claims to the Northwest Passage.
- In the financial and economic field, as when the Nixon administration put a surcharge on Canadian imports for balance-of-payments reasons.
- In the energy field, as when the U.S. government, some two decades ago, put our oil exports under quota, or, in the late years of the Trudeau government, threatened serious consequences over Canadian 'ex-appropriation' of U.S.-owned oil interests in Canada (the 'back-in').
- In the general principles of U.S. foreign policy, such as opposition to discrimination and the denial of national treatment (as in the case of Canada's petroleum-incentive grants under the national energy program).
- In the national-security field, such as the extra-territorial application of U.S. trading-with-the-enemy laws to U.S. subsidiaries in Canada (the Reagan administration's initiative concerning oil-equipment supplies for the construction of the trans-Siberian pipeline being a recent example).
- In the area of the protection of intellectual prop-

erty, as in the cable and signal-retransmission disputes with Canada.
• In the environmental field, as when the U.S. government refused to accept responsibility for environmental damage in Canada caused by acid rain.

In all these cases there is a clash of public policies pursued at the government level.

But a more common type of dispute has come to dominate and at times to overwhelm our relationship. This is the conflict that arises when there are no major, or even minor, principles or themes of U.S. foreign policy involved. Indeed the Administration is often not a player until the last minute or at all. The disputes are generated by a special interest targeting its initiative on a congressman, congressional subcommittee, congressional staffer, or regulatory official. These threats almost all arise from congressional initiatives and take the form of an amendment to U.S. domestic law.

With the vastly escalating costs of campaign financing, the rise of political action committees, and the almost automatic re-election rate of incumbent congressmen (97–98 per cent in recent years), Congress has become, as a White House counsel recently put it, 'the champion of the entrenched special interests.'

The impact on Canada is severe. In some instances, it arises as a spin-off from a change or attempted change of generalized application in U.S. regulatory regimes. In other instances, the congressional threat is a product of an initiative of a U.S. special interest aimed specifically at Canada; or it is an unintended by-product of an attempt by a special interest to use Congress to swipe at some other country or interest.

The congressional initiatives and manoeuvres that plagued my years in Washington only rarely involved the State Department or, for that matter, the congressional committees that traditionally deal with foreign affairs.

The first category of congressionally driven disputes arise from a rewriting of u.s. regulatory regimes. They are born of the fact that, thanks to technology, services are increasingly provided on a continental or even global basis. A prime example concerns the field of trucking, an economic sector of great importance to our two countries, given that approximately 80 per cent of our $200-billion two-way trade – the largest bilateral trade flow in the world – crosses the Canada–u.s. border in trucks.

The Motor Carrier Act of 1980 significantly altered the regulatory framework of the u.s. trucking industry, which became, in effect, deregulated; competition was the new order of the day. Entry into the industry became a simple matter. The applicant need only show that it was technically fit; it was not required to prove that its entry into the market would further the public interest. This meant that Canadian operators could take advantage of the new deregulated framework in the United States which, not surprisingly, they did.

The reaction of the u.s. industry was swift and sure. Before the year (1980) was out, u.s. truckers were calling for reciprocity, that is, for similar easy entry into Canada. But Canadian trucking is regulated by the provinces, and although some commitment to a lower level of regulation existed in Canada, the barriers were still severe. For example, to get a licence to operate in Ontario, u.s. carriers, along with Canadian ones, had to prove to a provincial regulatory body that it was in the public interest to let them in – no easy thing to do to say the least.

The U.S. Interstate Commerce Commission (ICC) had previously ruled that the existence of a tighter regime for entry into Canada did not constitute discrimination against American truckers, but a surge of lobbying unfolded, led by a powerful company, Yellow Freight, located in Senator John Danforth's Missouri constituency. The distinguished senator had become upset about the blocked entry into Ontario of the Missouri-based operator. Under congressional pressure, the ICC imposed a freeze on Canadian applications, but then, once again, found no Canadian discrimination.

In marched the Congress. In 1982 it passed the Bus Regulatory Reform Act, which imposed a two-year moratorium on applications for operating authority by Canadian (and Mexican) motor carriers. Thus, no Canadian trucker could get a new licence to operate in the United States.

After high-level negotiations, the crisis was diffused, the moratorium was lifted, and an agreement was signed by the U.S. ambassador for trade, William Brock, and myself in which both sides subscribed to 'improving the flow of commerce across their borders ... through the availability of market oriented motor carrier services on a non-discriminatory basis.' Ontario and other provinces liberalized entry and, pursuant to the agreement, disputes came to be dealt with in the newly created trucking consultative mechanism.

What one learns from this affair is that serious, even grave, trans-border disputes with Canada can arise when the United States, as a matter of pure *domestic* policy, deregulates an industry. In the trucking case,

49

deregulation led in time to discrimination against Canadian entry until, in effect, we agreed that *our own domestic* policies should follow in broad measure the U.S. competitive model. It is probable that the interests of Canadian consumers were served by the acceleration of our policy towards liberalized entry. But the alternative was to be shut out of the U.S. market – in other words, we had no alternative at all.

Throughout this period, the Canadian embassy engaged in the most intense form of congressional lobbying. The dispute was in crisis-stage, Canadian interests were being damaged, and one of the provinces – Manitoba – was well advanced in planning unilateral retaliation before the Administration got hold of the issue.

Lest one believes that trucking issues are now settled, it would be prudent to recall, from my earlier comments, one of my ten rules of the game for doing business in Washington – the Yogi Berra principle that it's never over till it's over. The United States recently brought a complaint against Canada because Ontario began temporarily to restrict permits for the new trucks that are larger than those made in Canada. The U.S. immediately began to consider retaliation.

A similar example of this type of regulatory conflict was also front and forward in my early Washington years. And, like the trucking issue, it goes on until this day. The dispute grew out of a proposed amendment to U.S. environmental law, again a matter, on its face, of purely domestic policy. But it had devastating implications for Canada.

In the early 1980s the Environmental Protection Agency wanted to ban completely the use of asbestos in the United States. Canada, a large asbestos exporter with major economic dependence on its production in Quebec, agreed that asbestos presented severe health risks in some applications, but was insistent that it was safe to use if strict health regulations were applied. The Canadian position was at the time – and still is – in complete harmony with the best international standards.

The Canadian asbestos industry hired some excellent lobbyists and, with them, the Embassy worked out an elaborate strategy to shift regulatory responsibility to other u.s. agencies that we believed would take a position more in line with the agreed international one. Eventually the Office of Management and Budget directed that the u.s. agency responsible for labour occupational standards – OSHA – should take responsibility for the issue. The zealots in the EPA, looking, it seems, for a quick fix, lost jurisdiction. The Canadian industry celebrated.

But then the powerful Democratic congressman from Michigan, John Dingell, intervened with hearings in his Energy and Commerce Committee, the domestic industries and agencies were able to regroup, and the decision was reversed. The EPA celebrated.

Again, too soon. Other players invaded the field and deadlock ensued throughout the Reagan years. The lobbying groups kept on celebrating.

Early in the Bush administration, the EPA issued an outright ban. Stay tuned in.

In the dying hours of the 100th Congress in 1988, the legislators were working on an omnibus drug bill. It was a bill whose goals we fully endorsed. We were concerned in Canada about drug abuse and had our own strategy to counter it. But there were some elements of the bill that caused us serious difficulties.

51

The bill tried to impose U.S. regulations on Canadians in Canada, for example, by requiring Canadian contractors doing business with the U.S. government to meet U.S. regulations for a drug-free workplace. Thus, if a Canadian manufacturer of toboggans in Montreal supplied them to the U.S. Army, the Canadian factory would have to comply with U.S. anti-drug requirements for behaviour in the workplace. We sympathized with the goals of the bill, I repeat, but we did not think it appropriate that the U.S. Congress legislate for Canada, extraterritorially, on how to handle the problem.

The responsible Embassy officer took our problem to the State Department, which referred us to the Department of Transportation, which gave us a good hearing. They sympathized and acknowledged that we had a problem, and agreed to help, but they also had some serious problems of their own with other parts of the bill. Effectively, our number-one priority was their number-ten priority.

We could either rest on tradition and propriety and risk seeing our interests damaged. Or we could go out on the field to protect them. It was not a difficult decision. We went out on the field. One of the key issues was to learn who was calling the legislative signals in the Senate. After frantic attempts to discover who was carrying the action on these extraterritorial clauses, I finally traced the action to Senator Warren Rudman of New Hampshire. Urgently, I had to pull him off the floor of the Senate. He listened patiently to our complaints and, to our pleasant surprise, understood our difficulties and was helpful.

Canadian lobsters provide the most current illustration of the regulatory game, U.S.-style. Lobsters beneath a certain size have now been banned from inter-state commerce thanks to the powerful Senate major-ity leader, George Mitchell of Maine. The senator, in a non-statesmanlike mood, voted against the Canada–U.S. Free Trade Agreement in an unsuccessful attempt to protect his lobster fishermen from Canadian com-petition. Not long after, at the end of 1989, he never-theless managed to get a law proclaimed in the name of conservation to accomplish his purpose. Canada protested and asked for an intergovernmental panel to be struck under chapter XVIII of the Free Trade Agreement. The issue: Is this a genuinely environ-mental-conservation issue or is it a trade-protectionist one? We lost.

Whatever the rationale behind the new regulation, Canadian trucks, lobsters, asbestos, or whatever can end up shut out, threatened, or restricted in the U.S. market by non-discriminatory, or so-called non-dis-criminatory regulations, often of a protectionist char-acter, initiated, promoted, and inspired by special interests operating in the Congress and passed into law, in one way or another, sooner or later.

The executive-branch role in these situations tends almost always to be reactive, limited in scope, and sometimes virtually non-existent.

The Canadian response in such situations needs to be fashioned according to the circumstances. Each strategy is distinct, depending on the source of the threat and the character of the players.

What is essential is that there be a specifically tai-lored microstrategy requiring a combination of public diplomacy, legal skills, alliance-seeking, and just plain old-fashioned lobbying. This will likely involve seek-ing out a potential ally in a U.S. industry that may also suffer if the initiative becomes law. The process will likely require the involvement of the ubiquitous lawyers, and the careful lobbying of Administration officers, committee chairmen, and each congressman on the key committee as well as congressmen not on the committee who come from adversely affected states. There will be protest notes sent to the State Department, and complaints made to the White House. Above all, and at all times, the Canadian industry affected will be urged to enter the fray, and play hard in the domestic game.

The other types of dispute that colour and dominate our relationship are those where a special interest seeks specifically to target Canada or another foreign country, with Canada getting side-swiped as a result. No more durable or irritating example of direct targeting against Canada can be found than in the field of border broadcasting. The dispute originated in a bill of the Trudeau government, Bill C-58, proclaimed in September 1976, which amended the Income Tax Act so as to limit the deductibility of the expenses of advertising on U.S. television stations for advertisements directed at audiences in Canada. The bill was part of a policy of strengthening the Canadian broadcasting system through capturing revenues that were escaping to U.S. communications outlets. (Note that I was no longer deputy minister of communications at that time.) Altogether, this law may have eliminated about $20 or $25 million of advertising from U.S. stations, although this was partially offset by the loss of U.S. revenues to a Canadian station in Windsor beaming on Detroit. How much of those funds got redirected into Canadian television advertising is a moot question.

The initiative produced the mouse that roared, a huge and tiresome quarrel over, in the scheme of things, a small amount of money.

Some u.s. congressmen were outraged, but the outrage was limited, by and large, to those with television stations in their areas. Senator Moynihan of New York, an outstanding liberal democrat and, in the view of many, possibly the most brilliant man in Congress today, was particularly perturbed. When I met him at the residence of the u.s. ambassador in Ottawa, Thomas Enders, in the late 1970s, I engaged, as I had done with Senator Claiborne Pell concerning East Coast fisheries, in an unproductive argument with him about our broadcasting policy. Senator Moynihan knew what his constituents wanted, as well he should. But the issues were to become dressed up in the language of protectionism, unfairness, Canadian cultural nationalism, and the like.

During the Carter years the Congress actually retaliated against Canada. Worse than that, they committed the sin of linkage. Unless Canada changed its border-broadcasting law, the Congress would not allow u.s. citizens to deduct from their income tax as legitimate expenses the costs of attending business conventions in Canada (and Mexico too, thanks to some other quarrel). We did not change our law, and Congress retaliated. According to Canadian studies, the cost of this reprisal to the Canadian tourist industry was a couple of hundred million dollars or so before the Congress got around to repealing it. The u.s. law was repealed not, God forbid, because it hurt Canada or was disproportionate – but because it was unpopular with American travel agents and the tourist industry.

Not long after the law's repeal and shortly after my arrival in Washington, Senator Moynihan, aided by the Republican senator from Pennsylvania, John Heinz, returned to the charge. To a mirror, tit-for-tat, reciprocating bill that would have made U.S. advertising on Canadian television non-deductible, a true zinger was added: any U.S. company investing in the Canadian communications video-text technology called Telidon would not be able to deduct its costs as a business expense. We feared this could hurt the product badly; we were still bleeding from the convention-expense linkage. But in this instance, we developed a microstrategy and it worked. Important American potential users, AT&T and the Times-Mirror Corporation, were not altogether amused. They communicated their concerns to the Congress, the amendment died, and the mirror bill passed in its original form.

Several points or principles are revealed by this experience.

1. The most effective way to fight a special interest in the United States is to find a U.S. ally in the private sector that has clout. AT&T speaks to any senator in the land with a stronger voice than the Canadian embassy. A public-relations firm the Embassy recruited at that time urged a strategy to find allies in Buffalo itself, possibly among the local business community that had advantageous interests in Canada. Always seek local allies, they told us, advertise locally, fight it locally. The strategy did not work for the simple reason that the Embassy didn't have any money to spend and doubted that effective local allies could be found.

2. The congressman that is the source of the threat may be a great liberal or a great reactionary. It doesn't

matter. Borrowing from Lord Palmerston's dictum, legislators have interests not friends.

Senator Moynihan was Canada's greatest ally in the fight against acid rain and for free trade. It is no exaggeration to say that his efforts in those areas made a difference from the standpoint of Canada. But our border-broadcasting policies angered him; nor was he a friend of certain Canadian fruit exports either. John Heinz opposed us on border broadcasting, steel, and other matters as well.

3. The narrowly targeted lobby is often more effective than broad-based economic ones such as consumer groups. The outstanding interest of New York – and Senator Moynihan – in electricity imports from Quebec was of no relevance or consequence in this instance. Senator Mitchell could never be persuaded by me or anyone else that the fact that Maine benefits overwhelmingly from Canadian tourism and manufactured exports to Canada might have altered his determination to vote against the Canada–U.S. Free Trade deal because of his lobster fishermen. The narrower the lobby, the greater the zing.

4. The microstrategies aimed at countering a congressman's initiative can become exceedingly complex and require a high degree of intelligence. By intelligence I mean, of course, not brain power but information, of which one can never get enough in Washington.

An initiative of Senator Barry Goldwater against Canadian cable ownership in the United States was skilfully neutralized by the Canadian cable-vision company principally involved. It enlisted the support of a body representing U.S. cities (one concerned about restricting competition), investors in the company's expanding American systems, and the powerful chairman of the Senate Finance Committee, Senator Robert Packwood of Oregon. The strategy worked and the bill died. The company, Rogers Television, could not have implemented this strategy without intelligence, that is, without knowing who its potential allies were. A good U.S. domestic ally is worth a hundred protest notes to the State Department.

5. Successful micro-diplomatic strategies often require recognition that a country's best ally may be a congressman or senator on a committee who has no real interest in the topic at hand. This is because the special interest has no involvement – and hence, bite – in his constituency. But his influence may be neutralized because of issues in the committee that do concern his state.

This was illustrated by a particularly troublesome piece of recurrent legislation – the Buy-America amendments to the Surface Transportation bills that periodically came up for debate in Senator Robert Stafford's Senate Committee on Public Works and the Environment.

The Republican senator from Vermont was a highly respected legislator, champion of the environment and foe of protectionism. He was always ready to do his best to combat embargoes on the import of cement for use on U.S. highways (although aimed mainly at Mexico, the embargoes hit Canadian exporters badly) or rules imposing a high American local content for rolling-stock, such as subway cars (these laws also were damaging to Canadian interests).

Senator Stafford was one of the very first to tutor me in the ways of Congress. On one early occasion, I spoke of an amendment to a bill before his committee, inspired by Senator Pete Domenici of New Mexico, to put the import of Canadian uranium under a heavy embargo. When I complained about the proposal, the Senator said he found it totally without merit; it would, he recognized, raise the cost of power in the United States. Elated, I said, 'Does that mean, Senator, that I can count on your negative vote?' 'No, Mr Ambassador, it does not,' he replied. 'But why,' I asked, 'if it is without merit?' Senator Stafford explained patiently that on an unrelated matter, ripe for decision, he needed the support of the senators of that region.

Some years later, U.S. sugar growers were increasing their squeeze on the rather modest Canadian quota on refined sugar. I made a strong effort to fight the manoeuvre, but there were a number of senators from sugar-growing states on the relevant committee. At the Embassy we drew up a list of all committee members from states not involved in the sugar industry. One of these was Virginia, so I called John Warner, the experienced Republican senator from that state, to express the hope that he would oppose the new restriction. Like Senator Stafford on the uranium issue, Warner had no sympathy for the sugar manoeuvre. 'So,' I said, 'Senator, can Canada count on your opposing this manoeuvre?' 'No, Mr Ambassador, Canada cannot.' 'But why, Senator,' I asked rather naively. 'Because, Mr Ambassador – and you should know this – tobacco always votes with sugar and vice versa. Perhaps you are aware, Mr Ambassador, that Virginia does grow some tobacco.' So I proceeded down the list with my next call, hoping for better luck – or better intelligence.

6. Congressional lobbying is a public activity. This

lesson much be quickly learned in Washington and never forgotten. The notion of discussing or negotiating issues with a congressman in private is ridiculous. This stands in such contrast to diplomacy with the executive branch – traditional diplomacy – that it requires enormous psychological adjustments for a trained diplomat to adapt to this style of diplomacy. I learned this lesson over and over again.

I found myself often talking about the need for 'public diplomacy' and urging the government in Ottawa to allocate funds to get our message across to the public on various issues at hand. But public diplomacy has one disadvantage: it can be expensive.

In the same year that the border-broadcasting dispute erupted again in the Congress, Senator Barry Goldwater of Arizona, as I mentioned, sponsored a bill in the Senate for mirror legislation, or reciprocity, in the field of cable television, where Canadian companies were making a very big mark at the time. The bill would have extended authority to the Federal Communications Commission to promulgate rules to prohibit foreign ownership of cable-television companies where there was no reciprocity.

When I called on Senator Goldwater – one of my first activities on the Hill – I was going to try to persuade him that his bill was unfair. The u.s. broadcasting system, I wanted to tell him, was not like the Canadian one: it was not under any threat of foreign influence and therefore reciprocating made little or no sense.

I was met inside his office by an array of television cameras. I was on television to receive a heavy reprimand from the celebrated senator, and was lectured on camera on Canada's protectionist, discriminatory communications policies. My encounter was a modest media event – perhaps not so modest in Arizona – and no more.

Some years later, I asked to see Senator David Durenburger of Minnesota about an initiative he was sponsoring in the Senate to condemn Canada for a countervail action the Ontario corn producers had taken against U.S. corn growers. Since this was the only Canadian countervail ever taken against U.S. interests, while they had initiated at least a dozen against Canada, I was perplexed as to why so neighbourly a senator would take so unfriendly a measure against Canada.

Now more worldly in my ways, I was ready for the barrage of cameras. Together with my highly effective aide from the Embassy, Jim Judd, who always accompanied me on the Hill in those years (he brought Clint Eastwood qualities to our engagements), I managed to manoeuvre some of the senator's captive journalists into the corridor to explain why Canada was so upset at his initiative. I was getting more sophisticated, but not so sophisticated as to anticipate the senator's next move. He and I had a friendly, quiet, one-on-one discussion in his office, and I explained why I thought his actions against Canada were grossly unreasonable and completely unfair.

The senator listened patiently and made no great effort at rebuttal. He then made his pre-emptive strike. The senator asked, 'Do you mind stepping into my adjoining office, Mr Ambassador?' 'No, not at all,' I replied, thinking that the office we were in was about to be used for other purposes. As he led me in, he said, 'I want you to meet some people who are pretty upset about Canada's actions. Corn growers from Minnesota.' I was facing about twenty of them, all burning with anger and all assembled in order to zing the Canadian ambassador.

I hope I gave as good as I got; I must have been pretty effective, since the Senate resolution condemning Canada, albeit in a somewhat modified form, only passed by a vote of 99–0, with one abstention. If this wasn't one of my more notable successes in the art of congressional diplomacy, at least I was still gathering experience.

I proved more adept when I called on the late Senator Edward Zorinski from Nebraska, at his request, to discuss the fact that Canada was exporting more pork to the United States than the u.s. pork producers thought was good for them – or us. This was at the beginning of the long and terrible saga about pork that continues to this day. The u.s. producers were subsequently to bring two countervail actions against our pork imports, one for dressed pork and the other for live hogs. They lost the important one – that involving the added value – but thanks to the assiduous senator from Montana, Max Baucus, the Senate obliged by amending the countervail law so that the u.s. pork producers could bring and win a second action against our dressed pork, which they promptly did. Canadian interests appealed this result to a binational panel established under chapter xix of the Free Trade Agreement, where they are meeting with some success.

When I entered Senator Zorinski's office, there were, of course, the required television cameras ready to relay for home consumption images of the tough senator ticking off the cowed ambassador. As I entered, I took some popcorn from the large bowl that he kept on his table as a mark of friendship to all who crossed his portals. Popping some into my mouth, I said to him - and the cameras – 'Senator, I don't know how appropriate it is for you to be summoning me to talk about pork.' The senator, somewhat taken aback, stammered and asked why. 'Because,' I replied, 'You are a Jewish senator and I am a Jewish ambassador, and you are complaining to me that your constituents are getting too much pork at too low cost. Now I ask you, is that appropriate?'

It took a few seconds for the senator to begin to laugh. I certainly won the battle of the headlines in Wichita: the leading journal carried the story entitled 'Canadian Ambassador tells Senator discussion on pork not kosher.' But we lost the countervail. As I learned, you can't win them all.

7. All this adds up to one critical point: there is no commodity more valuable in the new diplomacy than access. By access, I mean the ability to get to see the people who can hurt or help your country. And, as I have said, access is usually gained at the social level, so my wife and I always regarded the social function as a high priority in promoting Canada. In respect of the importance of the party, traditional diplomacy and the new diplomacy are the same. What is different in the new diplomacy is *who* you entertain and why.

While these various principles that I have just outlined apply across the board to all types of lobbying situations in Washington, the environmental field invariably has involved, from a Canadian standpoint, the most dangerous terrain for seeking to change attitudes and outcomes in the Congress. I found that the subject of acid rain engaged passions like no other and although one was dealing with the atmosphere, it often felt like hot water. My first lobbying experience with acid rain was a unique one that provided me with considerable insight into how the sophisticated U.S. system works.

I visited early one morning soon after my arrival the office of a distinguished, elderly senator from the coal-mining state of West Virginia, Jennings Randolph. He courteously invited me to explain the purpose of my visit, and while I bravely informed him why, even though from a coal-mining state, he should not fear acid-rain controls, he went through his mail and seemed to ignore what I was saying.

He then invited his aide to comment on my representations, following which he said, 'Mr Ambassador, will you do me a favour?' 'I will certainly try,' said I, perking up. 'Well, I have a dear friend from my home state who has a cottage near a lake in Quebec which he has visited every year for thirty years and which he dearly loves. This year when my dear friend returned he found his cottage was stolen, all of it, every stick of wood, every shingle, every piece of glass, even the hinges and doorknobs.'

'That's absolutely awful,' said I, in a mild state of shock. 'Did he go to the police?' 'Oh yes,' he replied, 'but they were of no help.' 'Why?' I enquired. 'Well,' said the senator, 'you see my friend didn't own the land.'

I soon recovered and said, 'Senator, the situation doesn't look good, but since you raise it, I'll contact the Quebec authorities to get a report and see whether anything can be done. Could you give me his name and address?'

'Mr Ambassador,' the senator replied, 'come over

here and sit by me,' pointing to a small chair behind his desk where he was sitting. Bewildered, I did so.

He picked up the telephone, dialed a number, and said, 'Sam, do you know who I have sitting beside me here in Washington? The Canadian ambassador, Sam, and he told me he's going to help you get your cottage back. In fact he wants to speak to you right now.' And he handed me the telephone.

Thoroughly shaken, I managed to stumble through the conversation and then, along with equally shaken aide Janice Thordardson, make a fast retreat out of the senator's vast, plaque-covered office. But the senator caught up with me. 'I'm just going down the hall to a committee meeting on the environment,' he said. 'And I want to thank you for coming to see me.' And subsequently I learned he described to the committee his interesting discussion on acid rain with the Canadian ambassador and spoke sympathetically of our concerns.

Out of a sense of delicacy, I will not reveal the name of the senator who had a request of a different kind when I went to call on him to elicit his support for our position on acid rain. The elderly legislator informed me that, some half-century ago, he had honeymooned with his now deceased wife on a beautiful lake in Quebec whose whereabouts he did not at that moment precisely recall. Would it be possible, he asked, to name the lake after his deceased wife? I realized my answer would require all the diplomatic skills I could muster. 'Senator, that's a provincial matter!' I replied. 'We in Ottawa have absolutely no control over the provinces.'

Such incidents aside, lobbying in the area of acid

rain was significantly different from fighting the special interests in any other area, and this was so for several reasons.

1. The Administration opposed the Canadian position on acid rain. So when we went to the Hill to argue for a treaty, we were seen as undermining a position of the U.S. government. When I lobbied against a moratorium on Canadian trucking licences, or banning asbestos, or quotas on our cement, steel, pork, uranium, and other exports, I was not fighting the Administration. Indeed, the White House and cabinet officials were often on our side. We were just doing their job for them, so to speak. They had neither the time nor resources to lead a fight on such – for them – marginal issues.

The situation could be more nuanced from time to time. For example, the Administration was a very hostile to our stance on border broadcasting – they believed general principles of fairness were at stake here – and didn't mind the retaliatory moves by Congress against Canada, but they were not keen on disproportionate retaliation. So this left us with sufficient leeway to lobby against the Heinz-Moynihan initiative.

In the case of acid rain, however, we were running four-square against a U.S. government position. For this reason, the charge of interference in U.S. affairs stood a far greater chance of being made.

The situation was made even more complicated because we were lobbying in favour of a change to U.S. *domestic* legislation – the Clean Air Act of 1970. This law established a domestic regulatory framework for improving U.S. ambient air quality. So it was unpleasant but not all that surprising to be attacked for interfering in U.S. domestic affairs, a charge that the U.S. coal lobby was not reluctant to make.

When I replied in writing to a vitriolic attack by Congressman Lukens of Ohio on the Ontario environmental record, I asked him if he would read my factual clarifications and corrections into the Congressional Record. He obliged by doing so, but then denounced me for this request. Then he also read into the record the text of a letter he wrote to Secretary of State George Shultz asking for my immediate recall on grounds of impropriety – interfering in the domestic affairs of the United States. (I never saw Secretary Shultz's reply, but he never asked me to pull up stakes.)

2. Given that the Administration favoured more research on the subject rather than a treaty with Canada, the issue conformed to the classic model of an international conflict. As it was more similar to traditional intergovernmental disputes, it became less acceptable for one party to the dispute to engage in public-relations or lobbying activity to subvert the strength of the other side's position.

This led at times to some strong criticism by the Administration of my actions on this issue. At the New England governor's conference in Providence, Rhode Island, in 1983, the combative governor of New Hampshire, John Sununu (subsequently White House Chief of Staff), exploded with anger after I articulated the Canadian position on the evils of acid rain. We were, he said, preaching to the United States about mending their ways while we were nicely polluting ourselves at home and not doing much about it. His point was: we didn't have clean hands, so we were not in a position to advise our neighbours on clean air.

As in the case of Congressman Luken's dissemination of inaccurate information, I answered his points with some vigour. My comments were repeated in the media and came to the attention of the then national-security adviser, Judge William Clark. He sent me a handwritten, not very complimentary, note about my behaviour at the meeting. I replied, saying Canada could not stand idly by in the face of inaccurate information being circulated about us.

Our relationship survived the event. But clearly, for a diplomat, I was manoeuvering in dangerous territory.

3. For some reasons that were never entirely clear to me, the Reagan administration seemed to adopt an ideologically inspired hostility to the idea of any regulation to fight acid rain. My first encounters were with EPA chief Ann Gorsuch. Before my departure I had received a word of friendly advice from Reagan's newly appointed ambassador to Canada, Paul Robinson. 'Don't confront the lady!' he told me. 'Try to win her over, if you can.' Good advice, but it didn't work. In my very first courtesy call, she confronted me in the style of a state prosecutor, reflecting her view that Canada was making trouble in the United States. I still recall my discussions with her with discomfort.

The ideological factor was very much present when I was negotiating the appointment of two special envoys to address the acid-rain issue, to be announced at the Mulroney-Reagan Shamrock Summit in 1985. The summit was preceded by the most exhaustive White House inter-agency review of U.S. policy towards Canada in Washington's memory. Front, forward, and foremost was the acid-rain issue. President Reagan wanted to make an important gesture to the newly

68

elected Canadian prime minister, but there was no disposition to change the official Reagan administration's position against acid-rain controls.

I lobbied the Administration by night and day to try to get an understanding that the first Reagan-Mulroney Summit in Canada would be seen as a total failure unless some cooperative step on acid rain could be taken in the right direction by two countries. Based on our approach almost a decade before to the East Coast fisheries dispute, I suggested that two special envoys be appointed by the president and prime minister to review the acid-rain problem and report to them personally with recommendations. The proposal became the terrain for a free-wheeling shoot-out within the Administration.

Opposition from the domestic departments to any action whatsoever on acid rain was almost overwhelming. The Secretary of the Interior seemed to find some credibility in the conspiracy theory, the Secretary of Energy preferred to leave everything to market forces, the Attorney General was sympathetic to the president's view (which was, it seems, that acid rain came from trees), the Office of Management and Budget feared vast wastage of money, and so on. The foreign-policy establishment, however, slowly got behind the envoy initiative, led by George Shultz with support from the president's national-security adviser, Robert McFarlane, and one lone player on the domestic side of the White House, presidential aide Michael Deaver. (He was later to pay a high price for his disinterested advice.)

While the battle raged, I was negotiating the terms of reference with a large inter-agency group led by State. The consensus in the group there was not even to admit that acid rain was a trans-border problem. After all, why start down a slippery slope? But at the eleventh hour, a deal was struck so as to give the president a decent position at the summit.

Most of the u.s. players believed that the envoy process would simply put off the problem for another day. It proved, however, to be something of a turning-point in the battle with the Administration. The two envoys recommended that acid rain be acknowledged as a cause of serious social and economic harm, which crossed borders between the two countries, and that a major programme be funded to commercialize the technology that could address the problem in a cost-effective manner.

Nevertheless, many high officials in the Adminis-tration remained unconvinced until the very end about the urgency or importance of resolving this problem. They continued to stonewall, and resentment ran deep because of the envoy process. In the White House, the Interior and Justice departments, and elsewhere, an anti-acid-rain position was, it seems, the last ideologi-cal stand of the Reagan administration. Reagan, in the view of some of these people, had given up on the theme of the Soviet evil empire and had gone far towards the wrong side on many issues on the conser-vative agenda. Hence, the wagons must circle to pro-tect the brave crusaders against any controls on acid rain.

The flavour of an ideological crusade could be found in important parts of the Administration until the very day it expired. It was left to the Reagan successor, regime's, the Bush administration, to reverse the Reagan government's stance.

There are, I believe, important conclusions to be drawn from the acid-rain experience. They are that both the method and content of congressional and public lobbying are affected profoundly by the position of the Administration on the issue at question. If the Administration is strongly opposed to the position of the foreign government, the potential is high for a foreign lobbyist both to increase resistance and breed resentment in the Administration's midst and to contribute to a backlash on the Hill.

Most important, insensitive lobbying tactics on the part of the foreign power can play into the hands of the opposing special interests. Such tactics are sometimes a gift to them. Over and over again, the coal lobby, the electric utilities, state representatives, and industry lobbyists tried to turn the issue from acid rain to Canada. The problem, they put it about, was not acid rain but Canada, and, in particular, Canadian interference in U.S. affairs.

It its more extreme form, this strategy was wrapped up into a conspiracy theory – Canada was advocating that expensive controls be imposed on coal-fired electricity generation in the United States so it could sell cheaper Canadian electricity. And meanwhile, the industry advocates alleged, Canada had not established any industrial anti-pollution controls themselves. 'Not one scrubber,' they said, did Canada have in its own territory.

Of course, we would point out that our sulphur dioxide emissions came mainly from smelters and you can't put a scrubber on a smelter, but our arguments were never accepted by the other side. Meanwhile, according to Michigan Congressman John

71

Dingell, the scourge of Canada, the Inco smelter at Sudbury remained 'the greatest polluter this side of the Milky Way.' (It was Congressman Dingell's hearings on Mike Deaver's lobbying activities after he left the White House, including those in respect of acid rain while in the White House, that led to perjury charges being brought against the presidential aide.)

In the light of the Administration's hostility, we adapted the methods and content of our lobbying in Washington. The Embassy at no time refrained from the lobbying activity, but we were on our guard, especially during the Trudeau years, when hostility to the Canadian government was at its highest and there was deeply entrenched opposition even to acknowledging the existence of the acid-rain problem.

As to method, the Embassy tried, whenever possible, to appear to be acting in a responsive fashion, talking to congressmen and staffers who contacted us for information or discussion. We worked closely with and strongly encouraged the private sector, especially the important and dedicated Canadian Coalition against Acid Rain, to be active on the Hill and take forward positions. But, discreetly, we continually initiated contact to reach important legislators who did not contact us. I called regularly and routinely on all important senators and congressmen with influence in the area.

As to content, we would maintain that our purpose was to explain the problem, provide information about Canada and acid rain, clear up misapprehensions about Canadian regulations, and rebut charges about Canadian laxity and insincerity. This approach allowed us to say that we were not lobbying against the White House, not trying to undermine the U.S. government's position, not playing politics American-style, and so on, and helped to provide a modest political umbrella to protect us from the heavy weather caused by the adversaries of acid-rain controls.

And, indeed, if we were not openly subverting the Administration's position, if we were not trying to tell the Americans how to fashion their own laws, we still had an important effect on the debate. We helped to establish 'the Canadian factor' – the importance of addressing acid rain as an element of good relations with Canada. There was more than one occasion when Senator George Mitchell of Maine or Senator John Chafee of Rhode Island or Senator Bill Bradley of New Jersey – all allies of Canada on the acid-rain issue – told me that it was the Canadian factor that, during the dark hours, kept the issue alive in the Administration and helped move it in the right direction.

Our strenuous efforts in Washington over the years, whether through lobbying, making speeches, disseminating scientific information, or raising the issue at summits, foreign ministers' meetings, parliamentary reunions, and so on, did help achieve results. Indeed, during the passage of the amendments to the Clean Air Act in 1990, an active proponent of acid-rain controls, Congressman Boehlert of New York, paid tribute to Canadian leadership. Acid rain is, perhaps, the only instance where Canadians have had a determining hand in the evolution of a major public-policy issue in the U.S. domestic arena.

The Canadian experience with acid rain demonstrates that there are issues that cannot be resolved without the active intervention, or more appropriately leadership, of the executive branch of the government. When the Congress is divided, as it had been for many years on acid rain, progress is virtually impossible. Special-interest gridlock occurs and there it can remain possibly forever, give or take a few years.

Canada had no hope of achieving a breakthrough on the acid-rain problem as long as the White House posture was negative. So Prime Minister Mulroney was right to put such overwhelming emphasis on the issue at each summit meeting with Reagan. He was right to make it the 'litmus test' for good relations with Canada. And, of course, we were right to lobby the Congress. But the notion, advocated by some devoted Canadian pollution fighters, that we should have disregarded the Administration and put all our efforts on influencing the Congress was mistaken.

This would have been a most dangerous course for Canadian diplomacy. Domestic laws and international treaties serve a common purpose and their architecture must be compatible. Canadian acid-rain law is in place, and now that new laws have been passed in Washington requiring U.S. emissions to be cut in half by century's end, a bilateral agreement binding the U.S. government and Canada now also can be put in place. It can provide us with an essential monitoring tool, both political and scientific, to observe, comment on, and, when necessary, influence the course of events as the U.S. law is implemented. The provisions of such an accord will be the touchstone of whether mutual undertakings are being discharged.

Notwithstanding all my emphasis on the role of Congress, we must not forget that obligations are placed on states, not legislatures. Canada's crowbar, our instrument to lever performance, our guarantee that neighbourly obligations must be fulfilled, our very locus standi as a nation derive not from the U.S.

74

Congress, but exclusively from international law and treaties. Even the most active lobbyists should never forget this fact.

Would I have predicted this victory a few years ago? No, I would not. Anyone who would attempt to predict with confidence the behaviour of the U.S. Congress is out of touch with the real world of Washington. But one point is incontestable. Without a switch in the position of the president himself, the Congress would still be facing gridlock.

There were, in my Washington years, other important areas of our relations with the United States where progress depended almost entirely or mainly on the stance of the Administration.

Recognition of Canada's claim to the waters of the Arctic Archipelago is an example of such an issue. Progress on the Great Lakes clean-up is perhaps another. Very importantly for foreign nations, the Administration can exercise its discretion in certain kinds of trade problems. Thanks to the generosity of Congress, which controls external trade, the White House still retains some modest measure of flexibility – for example, in connection with safeguard actions in the field of foreign trade. After intense lobbying on our part (one of my modest successes was to get the Canadian steel industry access to top levels in the White House), President Reagan spared Canada from steel quotas. Alas, he did the opposite on shakes and shingles.

Hence, in emphasizing the rising role of Congress in our bilateral relationship one should not downgrade the White House's leadership and intervention. On a number of the issues I have described, the Administration did come into the playing ground sooner or later. Nevertheless, one cannot get away from the fact that the Canada-u.s. relationship is driven more and more by Congress, that is, it is driven more and more by the special interests. This is hardly good news.

Foreigners might, in these circumstances, benefit from looking at the u.s. system in the following way. In the American system of government there is a king but no prime minister. The king's agenda must inevitably be small. Hence, it is impossible for the head of state to dispense too much attention on smaller, more marginal issues. The hanky-panky of special interests directed at foreign ones inevitably falls within this category. If there is no chief executive officer to combat the protectionist manoeuvres of the special interests, the foreign government is left to play more and more on its own.

The foreign government must recognize that it is at a serious disadvantage compared to other special interests for the simple reason that foreign interests have no senators, no congressmen, and no staffers to represent them at the bargaining table. They have no votes and no political action committees.

That is why a foreign government or interest often lives or dies by its capacity to find domestic allies that do enjoy these estimable assets. This leads some governments with an important stake in the u.s. economy to make a major financial commitment to lobbying, public relations, think-tanks, universities, publications, and so on. Although it is difficult to be sure of figures, it has been estimated by some that Japanese interests, public and private (is there a difference in this context?), spend as much as $250 million a year in such activities. Canada, the biggest trading partner of the

United States by far, does not play in that league. We should.

Is there any other way for Canada and other foreign powers to coexist peacefully with the u.s. Congress, and make our relations with the United States more fair and predictable?

One may speculate on the possible reform of Congress. But, frankly, foreigners should not hold their breath waiting for this to happen. It is true that as the clouds of the savings-and-loan crisis form over the Congress, the prospects improve for some reforms. It is the undisciplined and overreaching role of the special interests that brought on the biggest financial scandal in u.s. history. The savings-and-loan deregulation bill was, as aptly put by John Kenneth Galbraith, 'perhaps the single most ill-conceived piece of domestic legislation in modern times.'

It was these same special interests that were implicated in the political demise of the Speaker of the House of Representatives – the first quasi-impeachment of a u.s. Speaker in history – and other prominent legislators. Almost half of the House members received 50 per cent or more of their campaign money from the special-interests political action committees in the campaign of 1988. Speaking fees are still paid to senators by special interests. In that same year the average cost of winning a senatorial election was nearly $4 million; some campaigns went far higher, thanks again to the special interests – twice the average cost of a campaign in 1982.

Until the United States works out a system of public financing of congressional candidates, until it reforms some of the many procedures that allow special interests to manipulate the system to their advantage, foreign countries with interests to protect will have to struggle as best they can by playing in the domestic game with large handicaps. Recently there has been talk of a term-limitation for members of Congress – some suggest twelve years. This is perhaps the one reform that could reduce the power of the special interests, but it would require a constitutional amendment – no easy matter to achieve. While the rules will continue to change, I can, alas, predict with some confidence that significant reform of the U.S. political system will not come soon.

So beyond playing the domestic game, according to the current rules, is there anything a country like Canada can do to defend itself better against congressional threats? In the chapters that follow, I will examine the *institutional* route as an alternative to the microstrategies formed on an ad hoc basis to lobby.

3

The Administration and
the New Diplomacy

History, myth, and technology all combine to propa-
gate the idea of an imperial presidency, dominating
the u.s. political system and indeed the world. On
inauguration day in January 1989, I was giving a
course of lectures at the University of California at
Berkeley, having just resigned from my post in Washington. As I walked down Telegraph Avenue, I noticed
the headlines in a newspaper displayed on each street
corner: 'The Bush era starts today.'

This is not a totally inappropriate way for Americans to describe their times. After all, the Victorians
though of their queen as the emblem of their era. But
the English knew that their queen was a constitutional
monarch with very little power, whereas most Americans, and indeed foreigners, credit the president with
far greater powers than he actually possesses.

Events like the invasion of Panama and Grenada
and u.s.-led intervention in the Persian Gulf tend to
reinforce this notion of the all-powerful president.
They thus keep alive the images of the imperial presidency that took so strong a hold during the Great

Depression, the Second World War, the Cold War, and then through the Vietnam years.

Foreign affairs is one of the relatively few areas where the president does exercise substantial powers, but even these are heavily constrained. For example, President Reagan did manage to mount independent covert programs, notwithstanding the heavy congressional constraints laid down in the series of Boland amendments. But owing to these intrusive congressional constraints on military aid to the Nicaraguan contras even when provided covertly through regular intelligence modes, the president decided to conduct the operations – unwisely – out of the White House basement, and out of the reach of the Boland amendments. Thus the Iran-Contra affair was born.

Under the u.s. Constitution, the Congress legitimately exercises concurrent powers in the field of international relations and, through legislative power, has an overriding control over the actions of the presidency on the world stage. Indeed external trade, which is increasingly central to the conduct of foreign affairs, is a congressional prerogative, and the president's powers to negotiate in this area are delegated by the Hill.

The cliché of the Congress harbouring 535 foreign ministers is more than a cliché; it provides an insight into how the u.s. system actually works. During the Reagan years, the constant peregrinations of, for example, Congressman Solarz and of Senators Lugar, Laxalt, and Dodd in areas critical to u.s. interests – such as the Phillipines and Nicaragua – were in no way out of the ordinary. Indeed, they reflected the behavioural norm.

The deep struggle during the crisis in the Persian Gulf between Congress and the president over responsibility for the exercise of war powers is just the latest example in a perpetually unresolved tension between the two semi-permanent governments in Washington – the Democratic Congress and the Republican presidency.

The doctrine of the separation of powers, the central organizational principle of the U.S. system of governance, profoundly modifies the role of the executive power, in comparison with almost all other constitutional democratic models. For example, most legislation is originated in Congress and the drafting is done in Congress. It bears repeating that, in most instances, the Congress proposes, the Congress disposes. The president cannot even directly table a bill in the Congress; the Constitution does not provide for it. And when a legislator of his party does submit it, what emerges is likely to have little relationship to the original documents. And this is true whether one is talking about a tax bill, a drug bill, or a gas bill.

The highly important Omnibus Trade and Competitiveness Act of 1988, one of the most important U.S. laws of the past half-century and, in my opinion, one of the worst, was conceived, planned, written, and adopted by Congress. The Administration was not a factor in this debate until close to the very end, when, deploying the threat of a veto, it sought to address some of the worst clauses.

Notwithstanding these constitutional realities, the technology that now controls the transfer of information leads to an overwhelming focus on personalities. The Congress, with all its far-reaching powers, is an abstraction whereas the president is a personality, a father, a husband, a celebrity.

At about the time the presidential transition was about to take place in 1988, a well-known network personality and personal friend was transferred from the White House to the congressional beat. She confided to me that she greeted this transfer with some consternation, not because she failed to appreciate the importance of the Congress, but because, in the world of headlines, features, and celebration, the presidency is 'where it's at.'

Perhaps there was some consolation for the congressional press-watchers when, earlier this year, the Congress, for the first time in its history, in effect impeached its Speaker. The hapless Jim Wright was forced to resign for the sin of doing what every congressman has long been doing in one way or another – push the rules a bit to help him with his campaign financing. Despite the publicity attending the fate of Jim Wright, the similar fate of the Democratic whip, Tony Coelho, and the travails of the unfortunate 'Keating Five' (five senators under attack for trying to influence bank regulators), Congress remains a faceless, little-understood, unpopular, and secondary or subordinate institution in the minds of the American public.

Hence, the very nature of the electronic media presents Americans – especially the 80 per cent who say they receive all their information from television – with a massive and growing obstacle in the way of understanding their own system of governance. The focus on image, personality, and celebrity status carries with it the seeds of a great misunderstanding of how America is governed. It is the very nature of the medium of television to provide this focus on individuals – on the American 'royals' – because therein lies high entertainment value.

To revert to England, when reporters fill the tabloids with stories of their 'royals,' it confirms them in their celebrity status. But that is all it does. No one mistakes their celebrity for power. But in the United States, television reinforces the myth of unbridled presidential authority, obscuring the profound realities of American power.

The president is, of course, a prominent player in the vast arena of political power, but he has to share that power and pre-eminence with others who, depending on the issue, may exercise power equal to or exceeding his own. In domestic lawmaking, the president's role can be very minimal, confined on some key issues to the pulpit and to advocacy.

His one weapon, the veto – a weapon that President Bush is deploying more vigorously than his predecessor – is often unemployable because the offending law is tacked on to vital appropriations or other types of bills. In the absence of a line-item veto of the type most state governors possess, he cannot make his imprint on a great deal of legislation or prevent bad laws from taking effect. For example, some very bad new trade rules became law when they were inserted in the thousand-page Trade and Competitiveness Act of 1988 – legislation that the president was unable to stop for political reasons.

But even where the office of the Presidency *can* have an important effect on outcomes, power in the Administration is often as fragmented as the power that exists in the Congress itself. And, once again, appearances work to disguise the fragmentation.

The reasons for this executive fragmentation are complex. In the first place, in the U.S. system the president, as I wrote earlier, must be seen as a monarch, but not as a prime minister. In some ways, the president can be likened to a chairman of the board with no chief executive officer under him. For someone who sets the mood of the nation, who as formal head of state must conduct many ceremonial duties, who must establish the top priorities of the country, and sometimes act as commander-in-chief, the list of issues on his agenda must necessarily be very short. For this reason, he cannot be likened to a chief executive officer in the sense of one who manages the daily agenda of significant issues presenting themselves. A vast array of important issues must escape his personal attention or list of priorities.

My own experience was, of course, with Ronald Reagan, not a 'hands-on' president, as the world knows. So one could argue that one cannot generalize too much from Ronald Reagan's failure to keep his hand firmly on the White House switch, as often appeared to have happened, and not just in respect of the Iran-Contra activities.

But such a conclusion would be a mistake. Even the most hard-working and substantive of presidents, such as Jimmy Carter, always well into the files, could have but a short agenda, as we should well recall from the days when the Ayatollah Khomeini made President Carter a prisoner in the Rose Garden. Indeed, the Ayatollah was the cause of Carter's unfortunate decision to cancel plans for his one and only visit to Canada. Thus, a distant event prevented the president from attending to a task of a most high priority.

It is simply impossible in the United States to be an

effective head of state and effective prime minister at the same time. For the president to lead the nation, his agenda must be confined to the very broadest of goals and the fewest highest priorities.

In the second place, it is a fact of American political life that in the United States no one person other than the president can play the role of the prime minister. The president will try, with varying degrees of success, to fulfil a select few of the highest essential functions of that office, but invariably is unwilling to delegate to another the role of a chief executive officer.

One of the mysteries of the u.s. presidency is the unwillingness of any president to allow his vice-president to play this role. Given that the vice-president is the only elected member of the entire Administration other than the president, would it not be appropriate to cast the vice-president in this role? It would seem so, but it has never happened. The hapless vice-presidents, whether George Bush under Ronald Reagan or Walter Mondale under Jimmy Carter or Lyndon Johnson under Jack Kennedy and so on, are lucky if they get to play even an important ceremonial role. Remember the motto attributed to Vice-President Bush in the Reagan years: 'You die, I fly?'

Nor has any president been willing to support for long a chief of staff who de facto has the authority to be a prime minister. When I arrived in Washington in late 1981, the media were touting Edwin Meese, the president's principal adviser, as the prime minister, but that was their illusion. Donald Regan, in the second Reagan administration, confided to some that he was, in effect, the prime minister. That was his illusion. Under Dwight Eisenhower, a very disciplined man, his chief of staff, Sherman Adams, was regarded by just about everyone as the prime minister, but the enemies that he inevitably made brought about his downfall. And so on through history.

Again today, the subject is becoming topical. Is the former governor of New Hampshire, John Sununu, George Bush's chief of staff, becoming prime minister? And if he is, how long will he last? This aspect of the political life of Washington is unusual: the actors change, but the play remains the same. The consequence of all this is that even within the domain of his own administration the president's writ does not run that far or firmly.

Third, in the U.S. system there is no collective cabinet that takes charge of a wide spectrum of activities and priorities. The Cabinet consists of presidential aides – appointees – not politicians in their own right. In Canada we would probably describe them as bureaucrats and think of some as having a political bias. Nor is there any doctrine of cabinet solidarity. Before a clear and firm presidential position is taken, a cabinet secretary can take his own position on any issue – a daily occurrence in the Reagan years. And, not rarely, he does so even *after* a presidential decision as well.

Given the absence of a collective cabinet that governs the programs of the nation, the formal machinery that underpins the Cabinet is also less tight than in a parliamentary system. In the Reagan administration there were only two cabinet committees, one on economic and one on social policy, and often cabinet officers send subordinates to cabinet meetings. The result of this is a far less significant role for Cabinet in the U.S. system, compared to our own, in controlling the activities of the vast governmental apparatus.

Fourth, and closely related to what I have just discussed, is the fact that the U.S. cabinet and top officials are all politically appointed. Thus, in contrast to what if found in many European states and Canada, there is often a great discontinuity in the executive, lack of familiarity with the issues, and lack of government experience. Aside from exceptional periods, such as the Reagan-Bush era, the United States usually undergoes profound discontinuities every four years. Historical memory is often non-existent. There is sometimes significant expertise at the high political level, but it may be strongly influenced by ideological considerations.

Moreover, in recent years, the average time in office of the top political officials has been two years or less. In recent times it has taken a president six months or more to fill many of the critical senior posts. Indeed the period of time required to fill such posts has been getting longer in recent years, reaching new peaks of delay in the Bush administration. There is an element of countervail at work here. The greater continuity in the recent series of Republican administrations has led the Congress to fight back by an unprecedented harassment of presidential nominations, such as that of Robert Bork to the Supreme Court.

Moreover, the new political phenomenon of making sex and alcohol relevant considerations – a phenomenon hungrily exploited by the media – requires the Administration to investigate the private lives of the nominees in the greatest detail. Hence months are required to assemble all the necessary information – if one could so characterize or grace the kind of personal data collected. (Senator Alan Simpson of Wyoming once described it to me as raw sewage flowing in the streets of Washington.) It all leads to longer and longer delays in the starting-up of the new teams. This, of course, greatly weakens the efficacy of incoming administrations.

When all these characteristics are in play, it is difficult to generalize about their overall effects; but I believe that there are two primary ones:

1. In the absence of a strong and unifying political thread running throughout the president's cabinet, his control over high officials, even those not ideologically motivated, can be very thin.
2. The constant churning or turnover or vacancies that exists within the Administration makes for lack of continuity and more problematic control over the totality of the Administration's activities.

The dissipation or fracturing of power in the Administration is more than a mirroring of the similar tendencies in the Congress. It must be seen as an extension or projection of the fragmentation process in the Congress. Since the locus of legislative power on a particular question resides in the congressional committee or subcommittee, the committee also becomes the locus of activity of the lawyers, the lobbyists, and the vast array of actors on behalf of the special interests. Inevitably, they form links with players in the executive branch who are the object – and, in some instances, potential beneficiaries – of the special interests.

Elements of the Administration are thus joined with elements of Congress to form part of a lobbying-continuum in specific areas of domestic concern. Given the loose, or remote, hand of the president, or the White House or cabinet officer, the decision-making process in relation to myriad matters is slowly propelled by the force of specific lobbyists working on quasi-independent players in the executive branch who are interacting with sympathetic or compromised players on the Hill or in regulatory agencies.

Although the lobbying power extends deeply into the operations of the White House and Administration, the true centre of the circle remains the committed legislator, who is served by a very experienced and large staff. Senior staffers are as powerful as the permanent deputy ministers or under-secretaries in the British and Canadian systems, and certainly more independent and free-wheeling. These senior staffers provide continuity in the U.S. political system.

It is seldom realized that the members of the House of Representatives have had, in recent years, a 97–98 per cent re-election rate. The average congressman at this time has sat for some twelve years. Fourteen members have sat for over four decades, while many have been chairmen of committees or subcommittees for many years, such as the highly influential Sam Gibbons, chairman of the Trade Subcommittee of the Ways and Means Committee of the House of Representatives. The chairman of the House Appropriation Committee was first elected in 1941. In the congressional elections of 1990, 82 out of 435 congressmen were not challenged, except by a member of a marginal political party. Fewer than 50 or so had to meet significant competition. So congressmen are true Washington creatures, with the time and inclination to master the subject at hand.

Congressmen accumulate vast experience. Thus, while continuity and knowledge become overwhelming characteristics of the legislators on the Hill, the

Administration churns and churns, suffering profound discontinuities. This has been a key factor in shifting the weight of political power away from the Administration towards the Hill.

The permanent community of lobbyists and lawyers, public-affairs experts, and consultants understands this reality with perfect clarity. The 3,200 or so trade associations, employing – it has been estimated – some 80,000 or more people, understand it all to well. So do the 45 or 50 staffers per congressman. Add to this the 50,000-plus lawyers and the thousands of registered and unregistered lobbyists; they understand it too. The result is a vast permanent army camped in Washington and concentrating its lobbying attention and money raising on their favourite champions on the Hill.

The Administration's players in the field of domestic regulation, when drawn into this congressional vortex, often throw up positions that have less to do with the general policies of the Administration than with the claims of the special interests.

While the effects of the dispersion of power in the Administration most clearly manifest themselves in the domestic area, they can also be seen in areas where foreign interests are in play. In international relations, a surprising number of departments and units within the Administration play major roles: these include the National Security Council, the Central Intelligence Agency, the departments of State and Defense, Treasury, Commerce, Agriculture, Justice, Energy, and Labour, the Office of the Special Trade Representative, the Environmental Protection Agency, the Federal Energy Regulatory Commission, and so on.

For many years, the theory has been and remains

that the State Department has the responsibility for the coordinating role in the executive branch. But this is often just a theory.

Notwithstanding the enormous importance of trade in current international relations – unfair trade acts are a new form of international aggression – the State Department has at best a modest role in both the negotiating and policy processes. During the Canada–U.S. free-trade negotiations, for example, the State Department wanted to play a greater role, but was almost always kept in the dark by the Office of the Special Trade Representative. Similarly, important decisions, even far-reaching ones made by Treasury, such as those relating to international monetary accords, are beyond State's purview.

When it comes to actual coordination, it was overwhelmingly the pattern, in the Reagan years, for this to be done, if and when it was done, by the National Security Council staff in the White House.

If the Canadian issue involved important U.S. domestic considerations, such as acid-rain controls, airline seat-sales, restrictions on the import of shingles and shakes, the application of an antitrust law, defence procurement, restrictive immigration practices, protectionist state legislation, or trade-remedy harassment, embassy intervention in the White House might be the only way to get the issue out of the domestic department concerned and into a broader policy arena.

The description of this state of affairs is not meant as a criticism of the State Department on my part. Secretary of State George Shultz made an unprecedented commitment to Canada, and his proposal for quarterly meetings at the foreign-ministry level did more to enhance the State Department's coordinating role vis-à-vis Canada than any other action within memory. By setting up this informal but important institution, the State Department was able to keep watch on many of the troubling issues in the binational relationship that were the primary concern of other U.S. agencies. This enabled State to exercise, on a number of occasions, a monitoring or oversight role that they might not otherwise have been able to play. But it was amply clear, in issue after issue, that the role of the Canadian embassy was to take the issue directly to the Department of Agriculture, or Transport, or the EPA, or the FCC, or to dozens of addresses on the Hill in order to try to block a hostile initiative or defend a threatened interest.

Paradoxically, this dispersed and shared system of decision making in the foreign-affairs field can produce diametrically opposite results. When the issue is of major importance in foreign affairs, such as arms control or the support of an insurgency or whatever, the decentralized configuration of power can lead to a situation where, as Hodding Carter, a former senior White House official, once put it, 'There are too many hands on the wheel, too many charts in the pilot house and too few agreed destinations. That way lies shipwreck.'

Yet more and more often fragmentation can lead to another type of result: too few hands on the wheel, not enough charts, and a free-wheeling choice of destinations.

From the standpoint of a foreign country like Canada, the lesson is, however, the same in both types of situations. We would be far better off with an effective coordinating mechanism in the executive branch that can limit or constrain independent actors from making foreign policy in their own bailiwick without regard to the larger consequences.

The list of examples of actions taken, with little or no oversight, by a single U.S. department, agency, or part thereof, to the detriment of Canada, would go on at a great length. Here are a few I dealt with personally. In terms of foreign policy or media interest, none was glamorous, but they added up to billions of dollars and often involved important principles in the relationship:

• The abrogation of the fifty-year-old understanding on the entry of custom harvesters into our two territories – an initiative of the Department of Labour.
• The allocation of air-landing slots to the disadvantage of Canadian carriers – an initiative of the Civil Aeronautics Board.
• The banning of asbestos – an initiative of EPA.
• The blocking of acquisitions in Canada on the basis of U.S. anti-trust laws – initiatives of the Department of Justice.
• The extraterritorial application of U.S. criminal discovery laws in a banking context – initiatives of individual U.S. district attorneys.
• The denial of Canadian competitive access in various defence fields – initiatives of different branches of the Department of Defense of the military or naval services.
• Changes in the method of determining charges for the transport of Canadian gas – an initiative of the Federal Energy Regulatory Commission (FERC)

- New requirements for markings on Canadian steel products – an initiative of U.S. Customs.

And the list goes on.

Behind many of the issues of this type is an individual regulator or administrator acting at the behest of a congressman or his staffer or under direct pressure from a special interest seeking advantage over a foreign competitor. The regulator is a specific point of power located within the perimeter of the lobbying triangle – the celebrated iron triangles of Washington, unbreakable bonds forged among the special interest, the legislator, and the regulatory board or official.

It is often difficult for a foreign representative to pinpoint the source of the pressure behind the regulator. A case in point is the U.S.–Canada agreement on the free entry, for immigration purposes, of teams of custom harvesters to help farmers cut their grain each autumn. The agreement went back to the time of President Roosevelt and Prime Minister Mackenzie King, who signed it during the war years, and it came to symbolize our open border. I first learned of the closing of the gates from an official of the Immigration and Naturalization Service (INS) in Washington, who told me he was not particularly happy with the matter. I managed to learn in time that behind the INS action was pressure from the Labour Department. The Secretary of Labor told me he was not particularly happy about the matter; nor was the Attorney-General, whom I also lobbied. It took me longer – much longer – to discover that a particular senator was behind the pressure on the Labour Department. He also – need I say? – was not especially happy about the matter. And who was pressuring the senator? A particular union, but the information was a source of rumour and surmise. Presumably the union *was* happy about the matter.

In noting the limitations on the executive branch's capacity to control their own players in the types of situations I have described, I don't wish to deny that the president is a principal actor, or *the* principal actor, in respect of many important foreign-related issues. My purpose, rather, is to illustrate why diplomacy devoted to the executive branch must always be a part of a much larger strategy forged specifically, on a case-by-case basis, to address the issue at hand.

Canadian experience in major bilateral disputes provides ample material for demonstrating the need for both a focus on the presidency and the mounting of broader strategies. Among the almost innumerable issues that one could select to illustrate the nature of such strategies, I will deal briefly with three, each of which presents different but prototypical situations in the promotion of foreign interests in the United States: acid rain, free trade, and Arctic sovereignty.

The first, acid rain, is characteristic of a situation where the Administration is opposed to the foreign position or goal; the second, free trade, a situation where the Administration favours the foreign position without reservation, but where the active diplomacy of the foreign power is necessary to achieve the necessary wider support in Congress and among special interests; the third, Arctic sovereignty, a situation where the Administration really carries the responsibility, has the discretionary powers, and is dealing with a relatively quiescent Congress, but is reluctant to use its powers for broad reasons relating to the national interest.

The goodwill of the president is, of course, an asset of immense value to a foreign power. Its currency can be used in dozens of situations of which the president would never even be aware but where the White House, whether on the national-security or domestic side, can be of significant help.

As I mentioned earlier, I arrived in Washington at a time of great strain in our relationship. Indeed Secretary of State Alexander Haig, in 1982, wrote a letter to his Canadian counterpart, Secretary of State for External Affairs Mark MacGuigan, warning him that our relationship was headed towards crisis. It was widely believed that the two halves of the northern part of the continent were on fast-moving trains headed in opposite directions, one towards more and more interventionism and an expanded role for the state, the other towards deregulation and a shrinking role for government. This perception reinforced the strains and resentment caused by the Trudeau government's investment and energy policies, as exemplified by the Foreign Investment Review Act (FIRA) and the National Energy Program (NEP).

The tensions created by different or opposing domestic ideologies, if one can use that word in this context, were aggravated by Prime Minister Trudeau's criticism of Ronald Reagan's hard line on the Soviet Union and disarmament negotiations. These tensions came to a head in unpleasant exchanges or incidents at the Bonn NATO and Versailles economic summits in 1982 and were to remain a factor in the relationship until the resignation of Trudeau in 1984.

There nevertheless remained a residual element of goodwill towards Canada in the Reagan White House. The president, in his political campaign of 1980–1, spoke of a special trilateral relationship that the United States had with Mexico and Canada. In his mind there was a particular symbolism that attached to the relationship with Canada – that of neighbourly friendship in a troubled world.

Not long after I arrived in Washington, I heard from several old hands, like former U.S. Ambassador to Canada Thomas Enders and then Assistant Secretary of State Lawrence Eagleburger that the president's sentiment towards Canada (as distinguished from his attitude towards its prime minister) should be regarded as an asset and allow us to achieve a privileged position or special leverage in the White House, as compared with other foreign countries.

This residual goodwill may have been there, but was not really evident to my eyes during that period. I was more struck by the sense of anger and irritation at Canada's activist behaviour in the arms-control field and at what was seen as Trudeau's habit of putting the two superpowers in the same basket and finding them, or giving the impression of finding them, 'morally equivalent.'

There was some negative fallout from this in our bilateral relations, but it was not easy to assess. Probably the most significant evidence was the total collapse of negotiations between our two countries on acid-rain controls. The talks slowly died in 1982 and 1983 and were never revived in Mr Trudeau's time. The Liberal government launched an important bilateral economic initiative on sectoral free trade – and it too had little support in Washington. But that was because it was not well thought out, and it soon died.

Some significant protectionist actions were taken against Canada in this period – for example, our exports were constrained in specialty steel, cement, rolling-stock, and some other areas – but these restrictions were driven by special interests and were initiatives of the Congress, not the Administration. In any event, Mr Trudeau and his government maintained considerable popularity in Democratic circles on the Hill. (As Robert Strauss told me in one of our regular tête-à-têtes, Pierre Trudeau was a recognizable figure in the country as a whole – perhaps, along with Margaret Thatcher, the most recognizable.) The Canadian prime minister's strong and principled stance in 1983 in favour of Canada's testing of the cruise missile also won him admirers in both parties and in the White House, although his subsequent peace initiative was not well received.

A hallmark of the campaign of Pierre Trudeau's successor was the refurbishing of the Canada–U.S. relationship. Brian Mulroney called specifically for abolishing or drastically restricting FIRA and the NEP, which he proceeded to do after his election in 1984.

A centre-piece of the new prime minister's strategy was to achieve a better relationship with the U.S. president. It was at their first meeting, in September 1984, that Mr Mulroney proposed having annual summits between the two leaders. The idea of annual summits was something that I had personally urged on Mr Trudeau and the Cabinet, and while it was considered sympathetically it was neither rejected nor accepted. Mr Mulroney did accept the idea, the U.S. president agreed, and the annual summits became a central feature of the relationship between the two states.

The prime minister implemented with great success his strategy of having close personal relations with the u.s. president. Canada, along with Britain, stood at the very top of the list of favoured countries in the Reagan White House.

The meetings between the two leaders invariably led to massive preparation on both sides. The National Security Council took direct charge of inter-agency consultations. The policy review preceding the Shamrock Summit in 1985 was, as I mentioned earlier, the most comprehensive review of Canadian affairs to take place in Washington within memory. If goodwill mattered, Canada now had it, and in considerable measure.

Did it matter? Was there a benefit to Canada in standing high in the White House? The answer is yes, but it is an answer not without many qualifications and nuances.

The much-improved relationship between the two countries did not lead to the achievement of a bilateral accord to limit the trans-border emissions of acid rain. Throughout the entire period, President Reagan and his Administration remained adamantly opposed to such an accord. Prime Minister Mulroney single-mindedly brought great personal persuasion to bear on all occasions – more than had Mr Trudeau – when they met bilaterally, when they spoke on the telephone, and when they met at the annual Western Economic Summit meetings. Mulroney over and over again made clear that an acid-rain agreement was the 'litmus' test of u.s. friendship in Canada. He would ask very pointedly how a Canadian political leader, as a good neighbour, could be sensitive to u.s. concerns, as he was trying to be, if the United States was so insensitive to Canada's principal concern.

In the end, the presidential position could not be

reversed. Reagan, as governor of California, had formed strong antipathies towards environmental lobbies, had absorbed strange theories on the causes of acid rain, and was attended, at close hand, by advisers ideologically hostile to new controls on the emissions of sulphur dioxide and nitrogen oxides.

Yet the close personal relationship that the two leaders enjoyed was responsible for some modest but not unimportant shifts in the Administration's stance. At the summit meeting in Quebec City in 1985, Reagan, after furious lobbying on our part against powerful opposition in his own Cabinet and even within the EPA, agreed to appoint two highly respected political envoys – Bill Davis of Canada and Drew Lewis of the United States – to study the problem. At the next summit in 1986, Reagan, again after furious lobbying, agreed to adopt the Davis-Lewis report. His Administration thus officially recognized for the first time that acid rain did flow across boundaries and caused serious social and economic harm. At the subsequent bilateral summit in Washington in 1986, once again after the most strenuous lobbying on our part, the president ensured full funding for the coal-technology program, thereby reversing the inadequate budgetary allocation for implementing the envoys' recommendation.

What did all this achieve? The primary benefit of the report was to contribute to a growing consensus in the United States that acid rain was a serious environmental problem and needed to be addressed by adequate control methods. This was something less than a breakthrough, but more than a standstill. We moved the cause forward in a country where consensus must underpin any major and costly new national program and where it is exceedingly difficult to achieve because of the power of conflicting regional and special interests.

The acid-rain experience thus demonstrated the value of a close working relationship between the prime minister and the president, but it also showed that even a close personal relationship may not overcome entrenched interests or strongly held views. As I have already stressed, this experience demonstrated that if the Administration is not on one's side and the Congress is divided, there are profound limits on what can be done by lobbying on the Hill.

In the political situation that then prevailed in Congress, a situation accurately described as special-interest gridlock, there could be little hope of achieving a breakthrough by lobbying legislators. Nevertheless, that exercise had its educational uses. Persistent efforts by Canadian officials and Canadian environmental lobbyists to inform legislators, staffers, the media, and public audiences of the dangers involved in acid rain contributed in some measure to the slowly evolving process of consensus-formation in the United States. It thus reinforced the limited progress we achieved through the mechanism of the special envoys.

My diplomatic experience in dealing with the Canada–u.s. Free Trade Agreement was of a very different kind. Here was a Canadian initiative that was warmly supported by the Administration and by the president personally. Thus, at all times our two governments were working towards a common goal.

There would, of course, be many sharp differences between our two countries on particular substantive terms of the accord. This was expected, but what was not anticipated were the strong differences between

the two governments on how even to launch the negotiating process. Nor did I expect that the u.s.'s foreign
partner – Canada – would have had to rely so much
on its own intelligence and its own lobbying on the
Hill to ensure that the process did not go off the rails.
My experience in this area therefore demonstrated the
importance of active diplomacy on the part of a foreign
country, even when the subject at hand is a goal that
the United States favours strongly and is striving to
achieve.

When the prime minister launched the free-trade
initiative in a written communication to the president
in October 1985, he thereby committed Canada to
negotiate a comprehensive trade agreement. But the
president could not equally commit. Congress has to
be consulted and approve of the negotiations. For
Canadians and other foreigners, the u.s. Constitution
contains many surprises, and one of them is that Congress, not the executive branch, has jurisdiction over
trade. Article 1, section 8, of the Constitution clearly
stipulates that Congress shall have the power to
regulate commerce with foreign nations as well as
among the several states and with the Indian tribes.

Congress has in recent decades delegated negotiating authority to the Administration under certain conditions, while setting out substantive trade laws in
various statutes. The principal delegating authority
allows for what are called 'fast-track negotiations.'
Under the 'fast-track' scenario, the two houses of
Congress could vote only 'up' or 'down' on the negotiated agreement, that is, 'yes' or 'no.' They could not
amend it. Obviously, it would be completely impossible to proceed without congressional fast-track authority because otherwise an agreement negotiated

by the executive branch would be amended to death by congressmen and senators.

No sooner had Canada committed itself to the free-trade negotiations than serious division broke out within the Administration on how to proceed to obtain this congressional authority. Canada wanted an immediate response from the president. This would require an immediate notification by the president to the two houses of Congress, in turn triggering the start of a period of sixty legislative days in which the Senate and House of Representatives could say yes or no to opening fast-track negotiations with Canada.

There were some within the Administration who agreed that Canada could not be kept dangling – we being committed while the United States was not – while others, especially Secretary of the Treasury James Baker and Under-secretary Richard Darman, believed that negotiations should get under way without fast-track authority. They were of the view that the authority should not be sought until some later time when the mood of Congress was less protectionist, less enamoured of fair trade than of free trade. Their concern – quite legitimate as it turned out – was that fast-track authority would be denied on the Hill.

Yet, it would have been a fatal error to postpone the seeking of congressional authority, as negotiating without such authority would have created an enormous degree of hostility on the part of Congress. Indeed, they would have regarded it as an usurpation of their powers. But at the time, opinions on the matter varied greatly among the wide spectrum of players in the Administration, including the State, Treasury, and Commerce departments, the Council of Economic Advisers, the Office of the Special Trade Representative, the White House on the domestic side, and the White House on the national-security side.

My intense lobbying activities on behalf of a quick U.S. response placed me in the middle of these strong differences within the White House itself, illustrating the importance of the lobbying role even in a patently non-adversarial context.

The White House chief of staff, Donald Regan, believed that the mood of the country was in favour of fair trade (a code word for protectionism), not free trade, and therefore tended to side with those who were reluctant to invite any congressional authority at that time. He therefore favoured negotiating first and seeking fast-track authority later. The national-security adviser, Robert McFarlane, who, like Regan, reported directly to the president, understood that delay would put the Mulroney government in a thoroughly untenable position.

In November of 1985, I tried to convince Donald Regan that he was wrong, but I made little headway. I then went to see Robert McFarlane and found him angry because he believed my direct dealing with Regan rather than first working through him to build a coalition of supporters was a serious tactical error. I had, he thought, elicited a premature negative response at the highest level short of the president, thus reinforcing the preference for delay of Jim Baker and Richard Darman before an effective counter-strategy could be worked out.

Thus, the issue of timing proved to be as complex as a theological debate in Byzantium. But I believe that our lobbying was effective, because it convinced the Administration to put aside its reservations and, in December of that year, it moved for authority from

104

Congress to begin fast-track negotiations. The political demise of the Canadian initiative was thus averted.

This debate, and my involvement in it, was a modest warm-up for the near-disastrous debate that was shortly to descend upon us on the matter of the fast-track authority. Only this time, it took place in the Congress.

Although the White House had been perceptive in sensing the mood of the Hill on free-vs.-fair trade, they subsequently became over-optimistic about the outcome of the vote to authorize fast-track negotiations which took place in the Senate Finance Committee in April 1986. The Embassy's independent assessment had been more cautious, but not sufficiently cautious, as events proved.

A few days before the issue was to come up in the Senate committee, both the Office of the Special Trade Representative and the Embassy estimated that there were about 14 or 15 votes in favour of granting fast-track authority and 6 or 5 opposed. The very night before the hearing was to take place and the vote was to be taken I received a telephone call from Senator Moynihan warning me of a sharp change of mood in the offing. The senators had just agreed to meet alone – without staffers – in closed session the next morning before the committee deliberations were to take place.

At that early-morning meeting, a number of the twenty members of the senatorial committee, both Democrat and Republican, expressed anger at the Administration for not being tough enough to stand up to the Japanese and Europeans for what they believed to be unfair trading practices. Other senators had other grievances. Some wanted to teach the Administration a lesson for reasons that had no connection with trade; others wanted to extract concessions on issues on their own agenda, such as appointments to the judiciary. The meeting was stormy and bitter, and before the day was over Administration officials expected to lose the vote by as many as 15 or 16 against to 5 or 4 in favour. The chairman, Senator Packwood, himself angry with Canada over our stumpage rates for Canadian lumber, skilfully achieved a deferment of the vote and thus averted the disastrous outcome that Jim Baker and others had earlier feared.

In the week that followed, my own efforts and those of the Embassy were devoted to the most intense lobbying. We knew whom the Administration was lobbying and they knew whom we were lobbying. In the case of several senators, such as Republican David Durenburger of Minnesota and Democrat Spark Matsunaga of Hawaii, our lobbying played a significant role, as did our sustained and close working relations with Democratic Senators Bill Bradley and Patrick Moynihan, and Republicans John Chafee and Robert Packwood.

The positions of Senators Durenburger and Matsunaga merit special mention. Senator Durenburger had been unhappy about certain policies of Ontario concerning sportfishing which, he believed, were having an adverse impact on the economy of some Minnesota towns on the Ontario border. As I noted later, it is, perhaps, a little ironic that Premier David Peterson (later a vocal opponent of the free-trade agreement), whom I steered into Durenburger's office on a crucial day, helped to clear the way for the senator's positive vote on the granting of the fast-track authority.

As for the late Senator Matsunaga of Hawaii, he

proved very elusive and would not, for over a week, respond to my calls. He had committed his vote to the powerful Senator Russell Long of Louisiana, the Democratic minority leader in the committee, who was determined, for his own reasons, to vote against granting the fast-track authority. The Embassy, however, developed its own microstrategy to reach Senator Matsunaga.

I requested the Canadian Consul-General in San Francisco, who was responsible for Hawaii, to reach the governor, whom he knew well, in order to pass to the senator the message that the hundreds of thousands of Canadian tourists who flock to Hawaii in winter would be upset to learn that the senator was opposing free trade with Canada. I do not know what message precisely was passed, but I do know that it was highly effective. I heard immediately from the senator (who was genuinely fond of Canadians and a committed free-trader) who, with a little last-minute help from President Reagan, provided the positive swing vote that allowed the negotiating authority to be granted by the comfortable margin of ten votes to ten (sufficient, according to Senate rules, for adopting a motion).

Without our intense, relentless, and I would like to think skilful lobbying, it is questionable whether the authority would ever have been granted. Certainly the president himself was brought into the picture very late in the crisis. The issue could have been lost by that time had Canada not independently pulled out all the stops.

During the prolonged negotiating process that followed after the granting of authority, virtually all the senior and many junior officers at the Embassy remained camped on the Hill. At the peak time for the opposition, we counted some 31 or 32 senators tending to oppose the agreement because of the hostility of special interests in their states. I directed almost all my time to talking to key legislators and attempting to combat the efforts of various lobbies (uranium, coal, wheat, metals, and others) to oppose the agreement, obtain more favourable terms, or, later, reopen it.

Throughout the process, my impression and that of my Embassy colleagues was that on many, if not most, emerging problems, our own intelligence tended to be better than that of the Administration and that, without it, the outcome of the debates might perhaps have been different. That the Administration's intelligence was weak and their presence often barely in evidence was the result, I believe, of a number of the factors I have already analysed. The White House was preoccupied by matters higher on its agenda, such as the Iran-Contra hearings, arms control, and summit meetings with Chairman Gorbachev. The State Department had no role and in any event was always a weak force on the Hill; Treasury also had other preoccupations and the u.s. Trade Representative office was seriously undermanned, heavily involved, as they were, in the Uruguay round of multilateral trade negotiations, in negotiations on the omnibus trade bill, and in the initiation of trade actions against a number of America's partners.

In these circumstances, the Embassy regularly served as a channel between the Hill and the Administration on vital aspects of the agreement. Perhaps the most notable example came in the final days of the negotiations, after the determined Canadian negotiator, Simon Reisman, broke off the talks because of immobility on the U.S. side on fundamental issues going to the core of the agreement.

The key blocking points arose from the failure of the two delegations to agree on the definition of unacceptable subsidies and new countervail rules, as well as on anti-dumping rules and objective third-party mechanisms to settle disputes.

A week or so before the expiry of the congressional fast-track authority, congressman Sam Gibbons, himself a very considerable trade expert, telephoned to relay a personal suggestion. If the two sides could not agree on new anti-subsidy rules, why not agree to defer the issue, carry on negotiations after the agreement was signed, and in the meantime allow the proposed bilateral panels to review the application of *existing* countervail and anti-dumping laws of the two countries. While there were difficulties with this approach, this was an innovative suggestion and one that had the potential of saving the negotiations. I urged Congressman Gibbons, after I immediately ascertained Ottawa's reaction to the concept, to try to get Secretary Baker behind it, which he did. Nevertheless, the idea was rejected by the U.S. side, though it ultimately provided the basis for resolving one of the most formidable obstacles to the agreement.

In the face of constant negative comments by Senators Max Baucus and John Danforth about the prospects for U.S. acceptance of panels for binding dispute settlement, I urged Senator Bradley, with whom I was working very closely in the final days and hours, to take the lead in a senatorial phone-in to Jim Baker to make clear that the Baucus-Danforth views did not represent the sense of the Senate. Whether this initiative was effective I cannot say, but shortly thereafter, under Baker's strong and decisive leadership, the Administration reversed its position on the Gibbons formula and came around to a stance more favourable to Canada.

Secretary Baker decided that the United States was willing to discuss the Gibbons suggestion as the basis for a deal. In my discussions with Congressman Gibbons we recognized that if the existing national rules on subsidies and dumping were to be applied, during an interim period, by the bilateral institutional mechanism – the panels – then neither side should be free to change those rules, during this period, to the detriment of the other. This was a critically important point because if the existing rules were not, so to speak, 'frozen,' new legislation, coming into force after the agreement, could have amended the rules to Canada's great detriment and there would be nothing Canada could then do about it. Hence Gibbons and I talked of the need for a freeze in the status quo.

After Baker agreed to the Gibbons suggestion as a basis for resuming discussions, the Canadian political team flew down in a final bid to save the agreement in the few days still remaining before the lapse of congressional fast-track authority in the first week of October 1987. The negotiations immediately met with another impasse. While the Gibbons suggestion (it came to be known in Washington as the Gibbons-Gotlieb formula) to apply existing countervail and anti-dumping rules was acceptable to Jim Baker, the idea of a *freeze* on the existing rules was anathema. The Congress could never abrogate its sovereign right to change the law of the land, Baker told us. The impasse continued to the last day.

Since I am the author of this memoir, I will cast modesty to the winds and take credit, along with those in the Embassy who assisted me – Deputy Chief of Mission Leonard Legault, congressional liaison officer Jonathan Fried (like Legault, a lawyer), and trade expert Bill Dymond – for the idea that broke the logjam. Allow the binational panels to determine whether any new laws of Congress or Parliament would frustrate the object and purposes of the agreement – which was the progressive liberalization of our mutual trade. If the panels were to so declare, then the offending state had the obligation to change the laws, and if it did not do so, the offended state acquired offsetting compensating rights or the right to abrogate the agreement forthwith.

On the morning of the last day of the negotiations this idea was rejected by the U.S. side. A few hours before the expiry of the legal time available for the negotiations – and after the prime minster was informed in Toronto of their failure and the Cabinet in Ottawa prepared a press release to this effect – Jim Baker, demonstrating pragmatism, made a second lightning move. He reversed the rejection of the 'frustration' concept earlier that day by the U.S. side and the formula was then embodied in refined form in the closing hours of the night. Minister of Finance Michael Wilson went to the window in the room in the Old Treasury Building where we were negotiating and held his thumbs up before the crowd of Canadian reporters standing below.

In retrospect, it seems that a good deal of the difficulties we experienced during the long negotiations had to do with process. They sprang largely from the way the u.s. side structured its delegation. Its organization, in essence, reflected fragmentation of the Reagan administration itself. Every agency with the remotest interest was included within it. While headed by a capable official, it was, in large measure, an interdepartmental committee masquerading as a delegation.

The Administration simply declined to create a powerful super-negotiator to run their side of the show. Secretary of State Shultz had urged the adoption of such an approach, but it was not approved. This made the Canadian negotiating task far more difficult because the Canadian side was required to negotiate in a sense directly with departments that would have been responsible, such as Commerce in relation to countervail, for any impairment or curtailment of their own responsibilities along the lines Canada was actually seeking. And as for Treasury, its top officials insisted on negotiating matters relating to their own responsibilities off on their own.

Not until the very end, the last few days, when Secretary of the Treasury Baker took direct personal charge as u.s. chief negotiator, was it possible for Canada to strike a deal with the u.s. side. His vital contribution sprang from his direct line to the president, his authority within the Cabinet, and his ability to get the Administration to speak with one voice, whether on subsidies, agriculture, or intellectual property, and to reverse its position on key issues relating to dispute settlement.

Finally, I turn to a third type of situation, that represented by our dispute with the United States over Arctic sovereignty. This was the kind of issue in which the Congress demonstrated no great interest and

112

which, both by reason of function and tradition, fell mainly, perhaps exclusively, within the purview of the Administration.

Within that branch of government, the players were legion – in the Coast Guard, Transport, the Navy and Marines, the Chiefs of Staff, the policy side of the Pentagon, the State Department in various branches, the White House, and more. When I first discussed the voyage of the Polar Sea in 1985 with the under-secretary of state for science and technology, Edward Derwinski, I thought I was going to meet him for a 'one-on-one' encounter. Never will I forget the enormous crowd of officials in the room – some two dozen or so – most of them agitating for a hard line against the Canadian claims.

When the Conservative government broke radically with the political hesitations of previous governments and boldly drew straight baselines around the entire Canadian Arctic, thus cementing a Canadian claim to the vast region, hostility was wide and deep within the Administration. The issues confronted centrally the historic doctrines of national security of the United States – freedom of navigation and freedom of passage for warships through international straits. On a contentious issue of national security with a friendly neighbour, never, in my experience, had opposition been more sharp.

The United States to this day has not recognized our claims to Arctic waters as internal waters, but nevertheless the Mulroney government did extract an important concession from the U.S. in this area. This concession was contained in an agreement signed in 1987 which states that no U.S. ice-breaker can traverse the Northwest Passage without the consent of the

Canadian government (while purporting to be non-prejudicial on the sovereignty issue). As sovereignty is only a bundle of rights, the most important of which is control over the territory concerned, and as Canada did gain additional control over passage through the territory as a result of this agreement, Canadian sovereignty was significantly enhanced.

How did this happen? In my experience, the story is not a typical one in diplomacy. The impetus came from the top down. The Canadian prime minister dwelled on this subject – rather obsessively, one might say – at every meeting with the president and the word eventually went down in the White House and Administration that the president wanted to be helpful. And helpful he was.

The negotiations were taken over directly by his strong-minded and remarkably effective chief of staff, General Colin Powell. He presided over a large and unruly inter-agency group. Suffice it to say that Canada's negotiator, Derek Burney, our current ambassador to Washington, obtained a major concession, with little or no quid pro quo. I believe this was because the president had no ideological position on the matter and wanted to do something to alleviate the Canadian government's political problem. He did it because the Canadian prime minister convinced him that he should do something to help him.

There are those who dispute the significance of the agreement, preferring to think it was no big deal at all or professing to believe that Canada accomplished nothing. I am not one of them. But what cannot be disputed in this case are the following: (1) the president was the primary actor on the u.s. political scene on this issue, and (2) he acted because of his personal relationship with Prime Minister Brian Mulroney.

I do not hold out this case as a typical one in the annals of Canada–U.S. relations or Canadian diplomacy. But it serves to illustrate that if a foreign country can get on the president's small agenda, then the consequences of fragmentation of power in the executive branch can be substantially mitigated or overcome.

4

Beyond the New Diplomacy

My principal theme in this book has been the profound changes in the exercise of diplomacy in Washington in the context of the fragmentation of power in the Congress and the Administration. Clearly, only a 'new' diplomacy, focused on the current realities of power exercized by Congress and the Administration, can give a foreign 'lobbyist' like Canada any hope of success in this complex environment.

But are there methods other than diplomacy for addressing conflicts between Canada and the United States? In this chapter, I will analyse the potential behind two additional concepts or approaches for protecting and advancing foreign interests in the United States. The first is what I call the 'multiplicity-of-instruments' doctrine and the second is the use of bilateral institutions to address the points of conflict inevitably arising in so large and pervasive a relationship as that between our two countries.

Turning first to the 'multiplicity-of-instruments' concept, I mean, by this phrase, a policy of encouraging as many as possible Canadian officials, legislators, politicians, businessmen, lobbyists, and others from all levels of government to be active participants in the effort to defend Canadian interests in the United States. In considering this approach and why it is to some extent heretical, it is important to understand the tension that has for some decades underlined the Canadian approach towards the management of Canada–U.S. relations.

The Canadian government has traditionally had to cope with two opposing factors in the management of the relationship on the Canadian side. One is the tendency towards decentralization and broad diffusion of activity among a vast number of Canadian players. The other is the tendency towards central control and management in the Canadian foreign ministry.

In the Canadian public sector, the relationship is driven by hundreds of institutions and organizations in both the national and the provincial capitals, each interacting with points of contact south of the border. This has always been the case, at least in the postwar history of our relations. But as these relations deepened and became more penetrating, and as domestic regulation and intervention mushroomed in both countries, the number of direct cross-border contacts on the functional level also exploded.

A study of Canadian treaty-making that I carried out some twenty years ago, when I was legal adviser to the Department of External Affairs, showed that the United States was far and away Canada's primary treaty partner in every area of state activity. No other country came anywhere close to the United States as a partner to Canada in the making of international obligations.

118

I thought I had counted them all, but when I left that post to organize, and become the first deputy minister of the Department of Communications in the federal government I soon became aware of a vast number of agreements of a different character. These were informal, working arrangements between Canadian telecommunications regulators – in particular between the old Department of Transport (which then had responsibility in this area) and its counterpart agency in the United States, the Federal Communications Commission.

These informal interdepartmental arrangements addressed a vast number of conflicts, actual and potential, in the use of shared resources in the communications area. Most of them, indeed virtually all, were unknown to me as legal adviser of External Affairs, where one of my formal tasks was to oversee Canada's repository of our international obligations, the Canada Treaty Series.

It is true that most of these interdepartmental arrangements were probably not binding in international law. They were not authorized by specific orders in council and were therefore presumably not intended to be enforceable obligations. Did that matter very much? No, not really. After all, an overwhelming number of bilateral agreements in our Canada Treaty Series are in the form of exchanges of letters, memoranda of understanding, and other very informal types of international undertakings. Yet, one way or another, they establish the rules.

Given my earlier publications on Canadian treaty-making, which I had foolishly hoped to be seen as definitive, I made an effort while in the Department of Communications to survey the nature and quantity of these types of inter-agency agreements that were stuffing the files of that department. It became clear that similar products of direct informal dealings were to be found in the area of agriculture, highways, licensing, health, fisheries, waterways, environment, and virtually every other field of domestic activity. I realized it would be impossible to be even close to definitive about the extent of such arrangements, and so I contented myself with publishing an account based on a broad sampling.

What is actually recorded in memoranda of understanding, exchanges of letters, minutes, and technical documents represents but a drop in the ocean of informal trans-border contacts that have been taking place for many years. The reality is that, at any given time, there are thousands of points of functional contact at all levels of government operations at the federal level. There is a similar phenomenon occurring in various ways at the provincial level with officials of neighbouring states.

These functional contacts are the backbone of the conduct of many aspects of the Canada–U.S. relationship. By their nature they are multi-channel and self-initiated. The fact that many are virtually unknown outside the relevant departments is a reflection of their success. They represent in many instances the results of relationships long cultivated and sustained, of shared interest in serious social and technical problems, and of cross-border bonding.

The Department of External Affairs has always been rather uncomfortable with these relationships. The foreign ministry has tended to look upon the international units in functional departments as rivals of a sort, albeit in only narrow fields. But the main problem has been that External Affairs felt it did not know what was going on, could be taken by surprise, could be embarrassed by sudden media attention to a development, and so on.

The Department had a point. As the Canada–U.S. relationship left the more tranquil era of the forties, fifties, and sixties, and moved into the more turbulent years of the seventies and eighties, the conviction grew among its officials, and eventually in other central agencies such as the Privy Council and Treasury Board, that some form of increased control had to be gained over the sprawling, decentralized, and increasingly contentious relationship.

The sources of a number of the new disputes had, for example, been spawned in the very Department of Communications of which I had previously been deputy head. Canadian policies in border broadcasting, taxation of advertising costs in foreign-owned magazines, advertising substitution, and television blackouts were regularly cited by U.S. ambassadors in the 1970s as signs of an increasingly fractious and sometimes deteriorating relationship. The late U.S. Ambassador William Porter's outspoken public criticism of these policies created a political furore.

'Management' of Canada's biggest and most difficult international relationship became the new buzzword in official circles. Lengthy and ambitious documents discussing the need for, and methods to achieve, closer control of all aspects of the relationship became features of the cabinet agenda. Regular cabinet meetings were scheduled to discuss these ambitious documents.

This does not mean that External Affairs officials had an easy time gaining control over all the players on the Canadian side. Far from it. The Department had become greatly weakened in recent years as a result, at least partly, of lack of support in the Prime Minister's and Privy Council Offices. There was strong resistance in some of the line departments (those with specific program responsibilities) to a strengthening of the External Affairs role. There were also continuing anxieties in central institutions such as the PCO about External Affairs aggrandizing itself at the expense not only of other departments but of the PCO itself and of the Prime Minister's Office.

By the late 1970s, however, the pendulum began to swing back towards External Affairs. A consensus was forming that the secretary of state for external affairs and his department had to be given more powers to manage better the burgeoning, conflicted relationship. The fallout of the Trudeau government's investment, energy, and cultural policies on Canada–U.S. relations was so far-reaching and upsetting that External Affairs finally began to gain its long-pursued objective of being a true central agency for foreign affairs with a government-wide span of control.

As under-secretary of state for external affairs in the late 1970s and early 1980s, I fought hard for this increased jurisdiction because I believed passionately that it was necessary if Canada was to perform effectively in an increasingly adversarial relationship with a country ten times our size. I revived the idea of External Affairs as a central agency of the Canadian government, somewhat to the surprise and occasional disapproval of some in the Department itself, and certainly to the distrust of many in the line departments.

Why the idea engendered disapproval is hard to

say, but it may have been the result of a combination of factors: it was seen as something new (actually the concept went back to the 1930s and the time of the Department's heyday under its powerful under-secretary O.D. Skelton); and it was seen as placing the central focus on economic rather than political issues. It thus made the 'traditionalists' somewhat uncomfortable. Nevertheless, with the support of Prime Minister Trudeau and the secretary of the Cabinet, Michael Pitfield, structures were rapidly revived or created to allow the foreign ministry to perform a sharply increasing coordinating role.

The defunct Interdepartmental Committee of Deputy Ministers on Relations with Developing Counties (ICERDC) was resurrected; for the first time ever, a committee of deputy ministers on foreign affairs was formed; this was followed by a mirror committee of deputies of the Cabinet Committee on Foreign Affairs and Defence. All were chaired by the under-secretary of state for external affairs.

The primacy of External Affairs over the foreign-policy aspects of Canada's external-aid program was for the first time accepted. Remarkably enough, this had been a bone of contention between the two agencies for close to two decades – in fact, from the inception of Canada's International Development Agency as an independent entity reporting directly to the foreign minister. The separate foreign services of Immigration and Trade and Commerce were also transferred to External Affairs. Then the responsibility for trade policy was itself folded into that department. Lengthy documents spewed forth from Cabinet specifying the procedures to be followed and processes to be respected in all dealings with the United States.

Never in its modern history was the Department of External Affairs accorded more power in foreign policy or a clearer mandate to lead, coordinate, and control the relationship with the United States. Nor were the controlling and coordinating committees mere paper institutions. In the months prior to leaving my post as under-secretary in late 1981, I presided over committees of deputy ministers at weekly breakfast meetings to try to get a better hold on the u.s. relationship. At these meetings there were no substitutes for deputy ministers and they came alone. The deputy ministers of finance and energy were regular attendees. High policies were discussed and intensely fought over.

The driving force behind this passion for managing the relationship was the deepening tensions in relations with the United States. We wanted no wild cards in our deck, no unexpected manoeuvres on our side, no uninvited new players. The drive for better management was impelled by the need to play our cards better, to time our initiatives more intelligently, to establish our priorities more realistically, to introduce order, and to reign in the free-wheelers. No surprises, no shocks, nobody on our side getting out of line. That was the purpose of it all. But, paradoxically, the centralizing tendencies in Ottawa took place as political power was being rapidly decentralized in the u.s. system.

The decline of the presidency in the Vietnam-Watergate years, the weakening of the seniority system, the introduction into Congress in the mid 1970s of a younger, activist type of politician, the changes in campaign financing, the decline of party discipline, the rise of the independent, all-powerful committee chairman, the proliferation of congressional subcommittees and staffers, the new openness, the unrestrained growth of the lobbyists, the formation of a virtually permanent House of Representatives, the formation of the Third House of Congress, the discrediting of successive occupiers of the presidential office – all of these factors were contributing to a major transfer of power from the White House to Capitol Hill and to the decentralization and diffusion of power on the Hill itself.

But curiously, the drive to tighter management in Canadian foreign affairs was not impelled by the changing constitutional picture in Washington. Ministers and officials were only dimly aware, if at all, of the profound shift in power and processes occurring south of our border. To the extent they were conscious of the changes in power relationships, they attributed them to the personal weaknesses of the current presidential office-holder – Nixon, Ford, or Carter.

It can be argued that even if these developments were largely unappreciated and little understood by Canadian officials, the trend towards tighter management in Ottawa of the policies and the players was a happy coincidence. In time, it enabled the Canadian side to cope better with the Canadian mirror syndrome – in this instance, the decentralizing consequences in our federal system that would have resulted from uncontrolled contacts with the undisciplined, undirected u.s. side.

Centralization on our side of the border, it could also be argued, gave us an advantage over the u.s. side – the advantage that comes with knowing where one's priorities lie and pulling all the weight of one's players in the direction of those priorities. In this manner, we could better avoid dissipation of effort and the dangers of undercutting our own position and undermining our own strategies through bad timing or unforeseen actions.

Nevertheless, the virtues of centralized management can themselves be undermined if there is too strict a control and channelling of effort through too limited a number of players. Tighter management should not necessarily mean restricting the number of players on the field, but it can come to that.

When I started my duties in Washington I strongly approved of one of the long-standing basic principles of the tighter-management school – that is, that all Canadian activity vis-à-vis the United States must come together at the Canadian embassy in Washington. But as time went on and I came to understand better the phenomena of power dispersal in the U.S. political system, I became persuaded that, although management was essential, it had to be used to expand, not restrain, the number of Canadian players in the field. It may seem like an obvious point, but it was not orthodox.

By augmenting the players on the Canadian side we could reach out more effectively to the thousand points of light that President Bush subsequently spoke of, but which I sometimes came to think of as the thousand points of blight. While the ambassador and the Embassy, the consul-generals, and their teams across the country could in time reach many of the points of power in the U.S. field of action, there was no way they could reach or be in close touch with all, nor were they necessarily the best means or instrument to reach some of them.

Provided everyone sang from the same song-sheet, why not encourage parliamentarians to meet and lobby congressmen, why not encourage provincial premiers to cultivate the governors, senators, and congressmen of adjoining states? Why not encourage provincial delegations of legislators to operate on Capitol Hill in specific sectors? Why not encourage Canadian businessmen to seek access to politicians when their business activities could influence the politicians' constituents? Why not get Canadian businessmen to lobby their counterparts in the u.s. private sector and encourage the u.s. businessmen to use their political clout? Why not stimulate lobbying contacts by officials of other government departments? Why not encourage and endorse private-interest groups to make their presence felt in Washington?

I came to call this the 'multiplicity-of-instruments' doctrine and proposed it in a document I forwarded to Ottawa a year or so after I took up my duties in Washington. It did not meet with a warm reception. But when I finally left Washington years later I was more than ever convinced that this approach, untidy as it might be, was necessary and proper for coping with the atomization of political power in Washington.

The 'multiplicity-of-instruments' concept is certainly not an easy one to put in place and manage, nor is it a simple recipe for greater success. There are many serious hazards.

1. The players deployed or, put more accurately, deploying themselves, may not agree with government policy. In the Trudeau era, certain premiers spoke ill of the federal government's energy and investment policies, even while plying their trade on the Hill – not surprising, but not helpful or meant to be helpful to federal policy. Premier Lougheed of Alberta, perhaps the most effective of all provincial visitors, was well

known for rarely agreeing to be accompanied by the ambassador or his staff on important senatorial calls on issues where he disagreed with Ottawa. Afterwards, the American participants would courteously tell us what was said at the meeting.

2. The provincial players deployed or deploying themselves might occasionally undermine or weaken the efforts of sister provinces. For example, the Social Credit leader of a province trying to export electricity – British Columbia – was somewhat too anxious to distinguish his province from the efforts of a socialist-oriented Manitoba, also trying to market electricity in an adjacent American region.

3. The danger of 'triangulation' could arise in many other fields at different times when there was dissatisfaction by a provincial or even federal official with the line being honed by External Affairs and the Embassy. Even federal ministers might seek têtes-à-têtes and adopt an independent line with their opposite members – for example, in the field of defence. Or, in addition to making unaccompanied calls in Washington, a minister might work in such secrecy (as was the case for Brian Mulroney's secrecy-obsessed minister of national defence, Erik Neilsen) as to make it impossible for the ambassador or the foreign ministry to know what stance he was actually taking during meetings on issues of the very highest order.

4. Activities of the lobbying officials might in some instances prove an embarrassment. Not long before a provincial delegation of legislators arrived from Manitoba to lobby on the Hill against the controversial Garrison diversion project in North Dakota, two of the Manitoba ministers, including the head of the delegation, were involved in an incident in Winnipeg

in which the U.S. flag was burned during a demonstration against U.S. policy towards Central America. The activities of the delegation in Washington in that instance were singularly unproductive.

5. The personality of the minister or official with responsibilities in some functional area might prove to be a difficult or irritating one. On more than one occasion a top-ranking Administration official would hint broadly to me that our cause would be better served by my preventing, rather than facilitating, a particular ministerial visit. Need I say that the objects of such comments could not be that easily deterred?

6. The timing of an activity may be unhelpful even if it is a good one. Parliamentary delegations, usually all-party teams, like to descend when they wish – during parliamentary recesses and breaks – even when the timing could be viewed by our U.S. domestic allies as counter-productive. This was a recurring experience in the area of acid rain.

7. Intense or open lobbying by government officials or special-interest activists can trigger opposing U.S. interests to raise the cry of interference in domestic affairs – a common refrain in the area of the environment.

Notwithstanding these hazards, it was my firm belief that, as a general rule, the more the lobbying, the more diverse the players, the wider the net, the better the outcome.

The case for management, both by Ottawa and the Embassy comes strongly to the fore here. The instruments of influence need to be instruments, not arrows shot randomly into a field. The Embassy, in particular, must play a strong coordinating role and, at times, an orchestrating one. There are several reasons:

- The timing of parliamentary visits needs to be calibrated to fit in with the u.s. domestic state of play; in lobbying, timing is everything.
- Legislators should address key contentious issues – whether steel quotas or toxic wastes. They must be discouraged from dissipating their efforts over a wide agenda.
- They need to know what they are talking about – no small challenge.
- Business, not social activity, needs to be the order of the day – an obvious point, but not always accepted.
- Visiting delegations must, at all costs, speak with one voice. When in 1982 the ministers of three provinces and I called on the secretary of commerce, the late Malcolm Baldridge, to address the softwood-lumber dispute, the ministers deeply impressed the u.s. side not with their arguments, but with their unity.

All these are formidable tasks. At the same time, inevitable bureaucratic and even political tendencies to restrict or over-control activities must be firmly resisted. They reflect attitudes that are shortsighted and conceptually wrong. Let a thousand flowers bloom – Chairman Mao's dictum should be the preferred doctrine for our Embassy in Washington.

And this is so even in situations where there is no obvious pattern to the activities or even when disorganization occurs. The Embassy's coordinating role must at all times be respected, but it should not ordinarily be a blocking one. It is to better formulate and direct the strategy so as to achieve the best possible results.

After many years in Washington I had little hesitation in concluding that, notwithstanding occasional tensions and sometimes serious problems, more good than harm came from expanding the number of Canadian players on the field and allowing them, in their own personal way, to play the game. Over the years I saw many examples of the high utility of bringing new players into the Washington political era. Premier David Peterson of Ontario, an attractive political figure in Washington, may not have intended to help launch the negotiations for a free-trade agreement. But help he did by settling a long-simmering dispute between Ontario and Minnesota over the licensing of sport fishermen in the Lake of the Woods area, a settlement that removed one of the principal sources of Minnesota Senator David Durenburger's irritation with Canada. This improvement in our relationship was an important factor in the support of Durenburger, a key member of the Senate Finance Committee, in the critical 10–10 vote for the fast-track authority in April 1986.

The 'multiplicity-of-instruments' doctrine is, in the final analysis, an extension of the lobbying process. At best it is a way of inserting new people, new voices, and new arguments in the advocacy process in the greatly dispersed and fragmented U.S. arena of political power.

All lobbying by foreign entities suffers from one great disadvantage. No government, when the day is done, likes to subordinate a domestic interest to a foreign interest or foreign-policy goal. Because of the doctrine of the separation of powers and the attendant doctrine of the sub-separation of powers, special interests are able to obtain very considerable leverage in the U.S. political system. I have, in these pages, been at pains to show just how considerable that leverage can be.

But although other democracies do not have legislatures and legislators with the capacity to wield so much independent power, nevertheless all are experiencing the impact of lobbying by special or local or regional interests. In Canada itself, lobbying is demonstrating explosive growth.

Over and over again, special interests are capable of showing that their clout does not necessarily depend on their size. Skilful public relations, clever manipulation of the media, noisy attacks on authority, public demonstrations, highly charged accusations, sophisticated use of the legal system – all these phenomena can contribute to making a small or localized lobby a highly effective one.

There is ample evidence to show that a small, disciplined, highly motivated and united special interest can exercise more political punch than a large one, even of national scope, which is not well organized or targeting a single issue. Hence the dictum: the smaller the lobby, the more powerful the punch.

Governments in all democracies find it increasingly difficult to disregard or overrule the demands of groups. The very fact that a special interest is a collectivity tends to legitimize its demands. But difficult as it is in normal circumstances to suppress or deny such demands, it becomes far more difficult to do so if it appears to be done for the benefit of a foreign interest or power. Indeed, I believe it is almost impossible in a democracy for a government at any level or of any stripe to subordinate a domestic interest of any type, no matter how narrow, to that of a foreign one. Even more important, it is dangerous even to appear to be subordinating a domestic to a foreign interest.

In the United States, Senator Lloyd Bentsen of Texas put it well when he stated that the days are over when the United States will subordinate a domestic economic interest to a geopolitical one. What this means is that the u.s. is no longer willing to sacrifice an economic interest for foreign-policy purposes or the advancement of its national security.

The implications of this political reality for the management of Canada–u.s. relations are profound. It means that cross-border disputes are becoming increasingly difficult to resolve on virtually any basis. Most disputes between our two countries arise from conflicts in public policies on different sides of the border. The policies may be federal or state or provincial, they may be engendered by special interests, they may be national or local, they may be of general application or parochial. Invariably, they engage the media and public opinion.

Examples of these type of disputes abound:

- A national cultural policy in Canada conflicts with a regional economic interest in the United States: the border-broadcasting dispute.
- A national u.s. policy on regulation conflicts with a Canadian provincial one: the trucking dispute.
- A provincial Canadian policy to support a local interest conflicts with u.s. local interests not benefiting from similar policies: the pork and potato disputes.

- A Canadian regional conservation policy conflicts with a regional U.S. economic policy: the herring and salmon problem.
- A local U.S. conservation policy conflicts with Canadian ones: the fight over lobster sizes.
- Provincial environment policies conflict with state ones: the Garrison diversion saga.
- National environmental policies in Canada conflict with national environmental ones in the United States: acid rain.
- A Canadian technical standard conflicts with a U.S. one: plywood.

And so on down the list.

Whatever the form, these conflicts raise the same basic question. How can governments in intensely democratic countries resolve disputes arising from conflicts of public policy when these policies are strongly supported by public opinion in jurisdictions on opposite sides of a common border? The answer is: with increasing difficulty, as the record clearly demonstrates.

It took approximately fifty years to settle the dispute over the flooding of the Skagit River in Washington by a dam in British Columbia, a dispute that involved deeply entrenched positions on the part of the governments of British Columbia and the City of Seattle. Only after a prolonged new intervention by the International Joint Commission (IJC) in 1984 was a settlement finally reached.

It took about as long to settle the dispute over the Garrison diversion project, which pitted Manitoba against North Dakota. This dispute over the transfer of waters from one biosystem to another had its origins in President Roosevelt's days, and was finally put to rest a few years ago when the U.S. side modified the project for financial reasons. In this instance there was also an important input from a neutral board – again the IJC.

The border-broadcasting dispute, dating back to Canadian policies promulgated in the 1970s, remains unresolved. Disputes over aviation routes remain unsolved since the 1960s. Conflicts over salmon regulations lasted some fifteen years before resolution by a recently negotiated agreement. An acid-rain treaty is now at hand; it will finally take effect some dozen years after the two sides started negotiating the Canada–U.S. Memorandum of Intent of 1980.

This short survey brings out two key points: (1) The span of time involved in resolving bilateral disputes is considerable indeed – covering, at times, decades of on-again, off-again work. (2) Most recently – in the past decade – a vital component in the solution of some of the disputes has been neutral or third-party mediation of one form or another. This suggests some significant potential for the use of objective third-party instruments to resolve policy conflicts in the face of intensely opposing public opinions.

Against this background, it is interesting to note the apathy or even hostility of Canadian officials over many decades to the use of legal procedures or third parties in dispute settlements between the two countries. The first speech I gave in the United States – as ambassador-designate to Washington, at the Canadian studies conference in Lansing, Michigan – contained carefully articulated arguments as to why both Canada and the U.S. remained dubious about the value of bilateral institutions in the management of their

135

relations. This was a restatement of the traditional skepticism of the Department of External Affairs towards third-party involvement.

Why was the legal tradition so weak in the lengthening annals of Canadian foreign policy? For most smaller nations, the view has, for many years, been widely held that international law and adjudication serve to protect the interests of smaller and weaker states against the stronger powers, since it addresses the phenomenon of the asymmetry of power. Whether this view is supported by the evidence or not, there is little question that within the foreign ministries and universities of many smaller European and Latin American nations over the past century, the belief in the importance if not the efficacy of international law has been quite strong.

One can probably identify several sources of the Canadian lack of interest in or scepticism about the role of international law. First, there was the historic Canadian perception that international arbitration had not served our interests. In the nineteenth and twentieth centuries, it was a common Canadian belief that we were on the wrong side of a number of the territorial awards made by the tribunals set up by both Britain and the United States to adjudicate North American boundary disputes. The litany is to be found in the pages of our history and it spells sacrifice of Canadian interests by the metropolitan power, Great Britain, for the sake of international and imperial interests. That view took on the status of a historic myth and, indeed, that's pretty well what it was – a national myth.

The truth of the matter is that Canada fared pretty well in the arbitration of this period, for example, in the St Croix River Arbitration under the Jay Treaty of 1794, the Webster-Ashburton Arbitration of the Maine–New Brunswick frontier in 1842, the Oregon territorial dispute in 1846 recognizing the 49th parallel as the Canada–u.s. boundary, and the Alaska Boundary Arbitration of 1903, seen as the very apogée of the British sell-out of Canadian interests to satisfy rapacious Americans. No matter that most international-law experts believe that the award of the panhandle to Alaska was well founded in the documents and in law.

The desire of the British to placate American Pacific interests at the time of a rising Germany, Theodore Roosevelt's political thundering and threatening and the partisan political character of his three nominees to the panel, the casting of a negative vote by the British arbitrator Lord Chief Justice Alverstone – all these factors were more than sufficient to establish a powerful, enduring anti-arbitration state of mind among Canadians and the belief that Britain was a weak advocate of Canadian interests.

The conviction remained entrenched after the 1920s that arbitration and third-party intervention were not the best way to settle our boundary disputes with our powerful and, at times, jingoistic southern neighbour. There was a belief, it seems, that the basic asymmetry in power between the two countries would be reflected in third-party legal outcomes – a curious outlook indeed.

Certainly, it was also curious that in the sixty years following the First World War, when Canada took charge of its own international relations, there were only three formal arbitrations between Canada and the United States and none between Canada and any other country. All of them were of a minor character, concerning only non-vital issues.

The *I'm Alone* arbitration of 1935, concerning the sinking of a Canadian rum-runner in the Caribbean in which Canada received nominal damages, at least dealt with the substance of the issue. The *Trial Smelter* case, an arbitration of over ten years' duration, dealt only with the question of compensation, as the liability of Canada for pollution in the state of Washington was admitted, as was the liability of Canada for the flooding of an area in upstate New York in the *Gut Dam* arbitration in the early 1950s. With hindsight, we know however, that the *Trial Smelter* case helped to establish the first commandment of the international law of pollution – Thou shalt not pollute thy neighbour.

To rebut this negative Canadian attitude to third-party dispute settlement, one might, perhaps, cite the experience of the International Joint Commission, established by the United States and Great Britain as an imperial treaty under the Boundary Waters Agreement of 1909. While it is true that the commission was substantially used in the inter-war years to investigate boundary-waters issues and had a good record in making unanimous recommendations to governments, it never engaged in binding arbitration and fell into declining and irregular use in the years following the Second World War, each government seeming less and less willing to refer newly emerging problems to it for consideration and advice.

A second factor at work, perhaps related to the first and equally attitudinal, was a rather conscious tendency in the ruling External Affairs élite to be somewhat dubious about the importance and relevance of international law in the maintenance of world peace.

The UN Charter, it should be remembered, did not require any breach of law or act of aggression for jurisdiction to be acquired with regard to a dispute. Only the finding of a *threat* to the peace was necessary to empower the UN Security Council to try to settle the problem. The General Assembly's requirements were even more flexible. Hence the lawyer's preoccupation with rules, definitions of aggression, and the like could be set aside as not required to negotiate solutions or keep the peace.

The Canadians were very at ease with this style of multilateralism and they saw in it, and in the structures of international organizations, some form of countervail against the influence of our most powerful neighbour to the south. Lester Pearson at the UN General Assembly, with his gifted aide John Holmes at his side, engineering popular solutions at the expense, so to speak, of the Great Powers, is perhaps the classic picture of Canadian diplomacy at its easiest and most characteristic in the postwar period.

It is true that a long line of Canadian diplomats trained in the law did push hard for a major Canadian effort in the development of international law, and indeed our contributions, especially to the law of the sea, were not trivial. Yet it cannot in all fairness be said that these activities were, for the most part, in the mainstream of Canadian diplomacy in its glorious years after the Second World War – 'les trentes glorieuses,' to borrow a phrase from the French.

With one exception – the establishment in 1959 of the Canada–U.S. Interparliamentary Group – no significant bilateral institutional mechanisms were created in the thirty years following the Second World War. Bilateral consultative mechanisms, such as the Joint

Canada–u.s. Committee of Ministers dealing with economic matters established a few decades ago, quickly became moribund. Virtually all Canada–u.s. ministerial meetings in all areas have been ad hoc. The Permanent Joint Board of Defence has declined greatly in importance in recent years.

So in my speech in 1981 I was comfortable in concluding that, in the world's largest economic relationship, neither side had demonstrated much taste for using joint institutions to resolve problems. I explained this tendency as arising from a deep preference on the part of both elected and appointed officials in the two countries to retain direct control over the issues.

Still, there were certain signs, even a decade and a half ago, of a change of heart in Canadian officialdom. No longer willing to rely simply on discussions, negotiating, and trying to influence the u.s. side in some manner, the Canadian federal establishment, during the past ten to fifteen years, has shown an increased willingness to create and use a wide variety of bilateral institutions to help cope with the growing number of intractable disputes plaguing the relationship. These fall within several categories.

1. *Consultative political mechanisms.* In 1982 the foreign ministers of the two countries, George Shultz and Allan MacEachen, agreed to hold quarterly meetings to try to help manage the relationship. This innovation has proved to be a durable one.

How this arrangement actually came into being is instructive. Shultz, the u.s. secretary of state, had newly taken up his office, President Reagan having just removed his predecessor, Alexander Haig. Shortly after Shultz's appointment in 1982, Pierre Trudeau appointed Allan MacEachen to replace Mark Mac-

140

Guigan. Shultz had known MacEachen since their days together as postgraduate students at the Massachusetts Institute of Technology in Cambridge. The two men had some qualities in common – both were extraordinarily taciturn – but the main thing they shared was a sense of trust in each other. Not long before their appointments, Haig had written his 'moving headlong towards crisis' letter to MacGuigan and there was a growing realization both in Washington and Ottawa that the state of the relationship was, for our two countries, alarmingly tense. The new Canadian foreign minister invited the new U.S. secretary to meet with him in Halifax late in 1982 and it was at that meeting that the two, aided by their ambassadors and a few officials, drew up a very long list of irritants in the relationship. To MacEachen's query as to why we could not do things better and why the two foreign ministers couldn't stay more closely in touch, Shultz responded by picking up a slip of paper and sketching out in his own hand the terms of an agreement to meet regularly to monitor all the issues. Thus were the quarterly meetings born.

The consultative mechanism has now lasted some eight years, and several dozen meetings having occurred at regular intervals. Neither the United States nor Canada has established consultative arrangements of comparable effectiveness with any other country, so far as I am aware.

In an equally significant development in 1984, the then new Canadian prime minister, Brian Mulroney, and President Reagan agreed to hold annual summits, which they did regularly thereafter. Although President Bush prefers informal meetings to the more formal-style summits enjoyed by Ronald Reagan, bilateral summit meetings at least once a year are still continuing and are here to stay.

These practices have become, in effect, new mechanisms for better management of the relationship. They can be considered new institutional arrangements because of their departure from the past ad hoc type of practice and because of the durability of the process, the clarity of the mandate to review the key issues in the relationship, the breadth and depth of official preparations on both sides, and the importance the two governments accord to the process and its continuation. Experience has shown how annual summits and foreign ministers' quarterly meetings have both been utilized by Canada to advance its position on major issues such as Arctic sovereignty, North American defence, and acid rain as well as many lesser issues.

2. *Consultative functional mechanisms.* On a lower scale of political importance and of a distinctly different composition, three functional mechanisms for consultation have been established in recent years. In the late 1970s an *energy* consultative mechanism was created to bring together representatives of the most important agencies involved in energy issues on both sides of the border. In the 1980s, similar mechanisms were created in the *trucking* field and *communications* sector.

In all three instances, the composition of the mechanism reflected the wide dispersal of power on the u.s. side. Virtually all departments and agencies, public and private, involved in the sectors in both countries met periodically to canvass the issues facing the two countries, address major misunderstandings concerning each other's policies, and bring the two sides closer together where that was possible.

142

Of the three, the energy mechanism is of the longest standing, the communications mechanism the most tentative, and the trucking the most comprehensive in its membership and most ambitious in its role of bringing together the two industries. It is too early to say whether these still tentative institutions will play an important or enduring role in the management of the relationship. They are not decision-making bodies, nor do they meet at regular prescheduled times. The energy mechanism has met often over the years, perhaps a couple of dozen times, the communications mechanism (called the Niagara group) only on four occasions.

What makes these functional mechanisms of special interest is the fact that all of them grew out of intractable issues in our relations and that in each instance both governments thought it necessary to create them. Again, their prime role has been to bring together, into a single forum, the large number of players with different responsibilities and interests in the relevant field.

In none of the three areas did the governments believe they were creating permanent or even on-going institutions. But there were no other instrumentalities available to reach out to all the players. As the two governments can neither resolve disputes through traditional negotiating means nor effectively bring into play all the various players dispersed throughout the system, the mechanisms appear to fulfil a broad facilitative function in dispute-resolution.

3. *Resource management and dispute settlement agreements.* As noted earlier, the governments of Pierre Trudeau and Jimmy Carter in the late 1970s signed an agreement that would have accorded to a bilateral

commission the joint management of some two dozen or so species of fish off the Atlantic coast of our two countries. Indeed, management, in varying degrees, of virtually the entire Georges Bank fisheries, the richest in the world, was to be transferred to a joint body so far as its management, conservation, and dispute-settlement were concerned.

This was a radical agreement, going well beyond, in its sovereignty implications for resource management, the subsequently negotiated Free Trade Agreement. As I discussed earlier, the American Senate, not the Parliament of Canada, walked away from this agreement. But the very fact of its negotiation by the two federal governments was a clear recognition on the part of both that traditional negotiating methods for resolving the long-festering fishing disputes of the two countries could no longer be accepted as satisfactory.

To this day, the East Coast fisheries agreement, in its commitment to a joint institutional approach to the management of a common resource, remains the most innovative and far-reaching of any accord ever signed between our two countries. It stands out as representing a historical turning-point in the attitude of Canadian officials towards managing our relationship with the United States.

4. *Conflicts over maritime jurisdiction.* The two countries also began to show an increased willingness to use *multilateral* institutions to settle bilateral disputes. As part of the East Coast fisheries political package, Canada and the United States submitted the issue of jurisdiction over the resources and waters of the Gulf of Maine to a panel of the International Court of Justice. Never before had Canada been willing to ac-

cord to a third party, the World Court, the decision on so significant a boundary question, carrying with it, as it did, immense significance for the allocation of the mineral and living resources of the continental shelf in potentially one of its richest areas. Fortunately, Canada came out rather well in the arbitration of 1984, although Canadian maritime fishermen professed disappointment, at least until American fishermen began to holler louder.

Not long after, Canada also decided to invoke third-party procedures to settle a similar type of bilateral dispute with France. There seemed no alternative to resolve a long-simmering conflict over territorial jurisdiction between the waters of Canada and France around the islands of St Pierre and Miquelon. Consequently, in 1989 the dispute was submitted to an independent tribunal. (It is interesting also to note that a highly sensitive dispute with the United States over the sourcing of manufactured goods was addressed by a GATT panel earlier in the decade. Canada lost).

5. *The free-trade agreement*. This agreement was adopted against a background of increasing procedural protectionism in the United States over the past decade. More and more often, private interests were resorting to harassing their foreign competitors with various types of trade actions such as countervail, dumping, and safeguard activity. Motivating the agreement was the strong desire on the part of Canada to find a better way to resolve trade disputes than through unilateral domestic determination, bilateral negotiation, or resort to GATT procedures. Unilateral national determination, as in the softwood-lumber case, convinced Canadian officials and industry leaders that U.S. administrative procedures were becoming

politicized. Negotiating, ad hoc, in an environment of increasing congressional protectionism was not seen as a viable approach for a country so dependent on access to U.S. markets, while GATT dispute-settlement mechanisms were perceived to be slow and cumbersome and not binding in any circumstances.

The Free Trade Agreement's provisions on dispute settlement in chapters XVIII and XIX are more far-reaching than many Canadian critics have been ready to concede.

• The consultative obligations extend virtually over the entire scope of the agreement and thereby bring most of Canada's economic relationships with the United States into the ambit of a formal consultative mechanism.
• If one government declines to abide by the recommendation of a bilateral panel on a matter raised by the other government – and there are few limits on what can be brought before a panel – the offended party can take compensatory retaliatory action. This procedure, although designed as non-binding, goes far towards bringing a definitive third-party intervention into the substance of the dispute.
• Binational panel decisions on dumping and countervail actions arising from national tribunals are final and binding on the parties.
• Binational panel decisions on safeguard and escape-clause action concerning imports are final and binding.
• Decisions by the panels on whether new laws introduced by Congress or Parliament are compatible with the object and purpose of the agreement are final and definitive, enabling

retaliation by the other side if the decision is not honoured.

The conclusion to be drawn from these provisions is that, once again, Canada departed from traditional ad hoc methods for resolving differences with the United States in favour of formal dispute-settlement mechanisms.

Although the agreement is still in its early days, there is evidence of some gain on Canada's part. Although many in Canada were initially sceptical about these trade-dispute mechanisms, the panels have been very active, with over a dozen disputes winding their way through the dispute-settlement mechanisms. The vast majority of panel reviews have been initiated, perhaps not surprisingly, by Canadian producers. A number of decisions have been remanded, in whole or in part, for reconsideration by the American administering authorities. The determinations have been reached relatively quickly and inexpensively, reducing to some extent the uncertainty and cost that formerly attended appeals of the American administering authorities in the United States federal courts. The bilateral system is a major improvement over GATT, which, however, remains available to either party. Indeed Canada recently enjoyed the benefit of a favourable outcome from a GATT panel on pork. These innovative provisions have generated admiration among other countries and a number are interested in emulating them in bilateral trading relationships with the United States.

Paradoxically, the main criticism of the free-trade agreement among many Canadians has been not that the procedures are binding but that they are not binding enough. Yet another is that the binational panels are applying only national laws, not international ones. Addressing these criticisms would involve greater transfers of sovereignty – the one consequence that the critics of the agreement wish most ardently to avoid.

Those who roundly criticized the Canadian government for failing to obtain 'secure access' to the United States market, meaning in their view a complete exemption for Canada from the application of American trade remedy laws, were equally adamant that Canada's own sovereignty – its right to legislate as it saw fit – should not be imperilled by the terms of any agreement between the two governments. In effect, certain Canadians wished to restrict the ability of the American government to exercise its own sovereign legislative powers, while at the same time preserving for the Canadian government its own right to do so. To try to negotiate such an agreement would have been a patent absurdity.

In the broadest sense, the adoption of the agreement by Canada reflects a recognition that, in the management of our trade and most of our economic relations with the United States, more is needed than the traditional reliance on diplomacy, old-style or new-style (the lobbying style), to protect our national interests. The institutional provisions of the Free Trade Agreement, the aborted fisheries agreement, the arrangements for high political consultations with the u.s. administration, and the mechanisms for reaching out to the extended number of u.s. players in different functional areas all seem to reflect a recognition by Canadian officialdom that the greater use of bilateral institutions in the Canada–U.S. relationship is an idea whose time has finally come.

The dispersal of power in the United States and the increasing difficulty of resolving bilateral conflicts are the forces that underlie the changing Canadian attitude towards managing our relations with the U.S. They explain the growing Canadian theme of seeking new ways to reach out to more domestic players and involve more third-party intervention in the political process.

In the years ahead it is very likely that Canada will seek additional ways to make greater use of third-party techniques. Indeed we will have to. As the weaker of the two countries, both economically and politically, Canada stands to gain by a larger use of independent mechanisms and by invoking more precise common rules of international trade.

In the trade and economic area, agreement on a definition of permissible subsidies will do much to make third-party settlement more predictable and fair and to reduce procedural harassments. The Free Trade Agreement established a maximum period of seven years from its entry into force to reach an accord on trade subsidies and trade-law remedies. Although this is not the commonly held view, the truth of the matter is that the lack of a common definition of permissible subsidies is more troublesome to Canada than to the United States. Ours is by far the more vulnerable of the two economies to trade harassment and delaying procedural interventions. It is therefore in Canada's interest to expedite the current bilateral negotiations on subsidies in order to make the binational arbitration process more fair and predictable.

Similarly, Canada will, in all probability, seek the creation of new binational institutions in the environmental field. Our two countries share but one environment, whether it is the air we breathe, the oceans that surround us, or the Great Lakes and waterways that divide us. A bilateral acid-rain accord, to be effective, must be monitored. Objective standards must be put into play to measure whether both sides are honouring their obligations. And objective tribunals should be established to see to it that the obligations are not violated.

In other economic and resource areas, and in the service sectors as well, Canadian interests will probably also be well served by creating, over time, new binational mechanisms and institutions. They could prove useful in reaching out to the widening number of players on the U.S. side and for injecting more objective decision making into the political arena as a way of avoiding bias or paralysis in the resolution of disputes.

For all these reasons, I am reasonably confident that the greater use of binational institutions in the Canada–U.S. relationship is both desirable and inevitable. There will be political objection to this approach on both sides of the border based on imagined infringements of sovereignty and fear of loss of political control. But for Canada, at any rate, it is better to have clear rules and fair-minded referees on the playing field than to be scrambling on someone else's terrain and playing, as often as not, according to their rules and without any referees at all.

But even if I am right and we will see greater dependence on such mechanisms in the future, substantial use will also have to be made of all existing methods and techniques for advancing and protecting our interests in the United States. The new diplomacy will continue to be the workhorse of the Canadian team. Lobbying on an ad hoc basis at all levels, and putting into play different lobbying strategies to fit different situations, will continue for a long time to be the principal way Canada advances its interests in the United States.

As a part of this effort, a greater and more liberal use by Canada of a multiplicity of actors will become increasingly desirable. Canadians must be prepared to deal with the dispersal of American political power through as wide as possible a deployment of Canadian players on the U.S. field.

The U.S. political system will not become more simple in the years ahead. Power will not be centralized. The doctrine of the separation of powers, with all its attendant consequences, will not be altered. Without major reforms in campaign financing, members of Congress will not become less beholden to the army of special interests that drive the legislative process in Washington. Even in the face of major economic disasters directly attributable to the overreaching political power of the special interests, such as the savings-and-loan débâcle, structural reforms of a far-reaching character are, in my opinion, highly unlikely to occur.

Subinfeudation will continue to characterize the exercise of political power in Washington. But, perhaps even more important, the process of subinfeudation will devolve increasing amounts of power from the federal government to the individual states. The ideological zest that powered the transfer of federal powers to the states in the Reagan years will not

151

drive the process. Rather, the incapacity of the federal authority to deal effectively with many types of economic and social issues makes the continuing process of delegation irreversible. This means bigger and more aggressive bureaucracies in key states such as California, the locus of such Canada–U.S. disputes as those over unitary taxation and shakes and shingles (the use of which the City of Los Angeles has now banned). Indeed, the growth rate of legislative bills at the state level far exceeds that at the federal level.

An interdependent Canada will accordingly have to continue to grapple with a political system of unmatched complexity as far into the future as the eye can see. For all these reasons, there will be no breakthroughs, in the years ahead, in the way our two countries adjust their differences and resolve their conflicts.

It is therefore in Canada's national interest to continue always to search for better ways to manage our relations with the United States. Canadians must be open-minded and flexible about the process of dealing with our principal international partner.

In reaching new agreements to settle disputes by arbitration, judicial, or other third-party means, Canadians should not be preoccupied with slogans about infringements of sovereignty. After all, we are witnessing, in Europe, the greatest voluntary transfer of sovereignty in history. The key issue is not whether sovereignty is being transferred but whether one nation's sovereignty is being subordinated to that of another.

Treaties freely negotiated that impose obligations equally on the parties do not normally prejudice a nation's sovereignty. The establishment of joint panels or tribunals to settle disputes involves some pooling of sovereignty by each party for specific purposes, but there is no subordination of power by one country to the other. Indeed, to borrow that ever-so-popular phrase of the u.s. Congress, the playing field is levelled. To the extent that the pooling of sovereignty results in reduced risk or threat of harm to the interest of the party concerned, the national interest is furthered and the national welfare enhanced.

Traditional diplomacy has given way to the new diplomacy. The new diplomacy, in turn, will need to adapt to changing situations and challenges. Beyond diplomacy, the realm of law and international institutions beckons us as a terrain to explore and upon which to build. To the extent we can succeed, the ways in which our two countries settle their disputes will serve as a model for the conduct of international relations among other states. Canadians should not be timid in addressing the challenge.

Index

acid rain, Canada–U.S. dispute over: lobbying efforts of Canada in, 63–74; as involving changes to U.S. domestic legislation, 66–7, 73; position of U.S. administration in, 67–70, 95, 99–101

Adams, Sherman, 85

Administration (executive branch of U.S. government): discontinuities of , 87, 88; fragmentation of power in, 83–8, 90; as object of special-interest groups, 88–90; role of Cabinet within, 86–7. *See also* president, State Department

Alverstone, Richard, Lord, 137

ambassador, guides to action in Washington, 34–8; as title in United States, 3–7; mentioned in U.S. Constitution, 3; as lobbyist in Washington, 8, 9, 22; relations of with Congress, 22; accreditation of in Washington, 30–1

Arctic sovereignty, Canada–U.S. dispute over, 75, 95, 112–15

asbestos. *See* disputes

Baker, James, 103, 104, 106, 109–10, 111, 112

Baldridge, Malcolm, 130

Baucus, Max, 62, 109

Bentsen, Lloyd, 133

Berra, Yogi, 37, 50

bilateral institutions. *See* dispute settlement

Boehlert, Sherwood, 73

border broadcasting, Canada–U.S. dispute over, 54–6, 57–8, 60–1, 135

Bork, Robert, 87

boundary-water disputes, Canada–U.S., 134–5

Brademas, John, 35

Bradley, Bill, 73, 106, 109

Brock, William, 49

Burney, Derek, 114

Bush, George, 40, 79, 83, 85, 86, 126, 141

Cabinet, in U.S. administration, 86–7

Cadieux, Marcel, 18, 39

Canada–U.S. Free Trade Agreement, 25, 53, 57, 62; negotiation of: 101–12; support of U.S. administration for, 95, 101; role of Congress in negotiation of, 102; 'fast-track' negotiating authority for sought in Congress, 102–7; role of president in negotiation of, 107; role of Canadian Embassy staff in lobbying for, 107–8; anti-subsidy, anti-dumping, and countervail rules as affecting, 109–10; dispute settlement under, 109–11, 145–8, 149

Canada–U.S. relations in the 1980s, 96–9

Canadian Coalition on Acid Rain, 72

Carter, Hodding, 92

Carter, Jimmy, 18, 23, 84, 85, 143

Chafee, John, 36, 73, 106

Clark, William, 68

Coelho, Tony, 82

Congress, Third House of, 32–3

Congress, United States: and conduct of foreign affairs, 27, 80; 'imperial,' 27; decentralizing of power in, 27, 29; as initiator of legislation, 28, 81; executive powers of, 28; use of domestic laws for foreign goals by, 28–9; powers and image of, contrasted with presidency, 81–2; prerogatives of regarding external trade, 80, 102; staffers for, 33, 89; changes in rules of, 39–40; experience of members of, 89–90; re-election rate of incumbents in, 47, 89; as champion of special interests, 47; as forum for regulatory disputes with Canada, 48; possible reform of, 77, 78

Constitution, United States: as unlikely to change, 39; as defining political context of diplomacy, 39, 40

Cutler, Lloyd, 18, 39

Danforth, John, 49, 109

Darman, Richard, 103, 104

Davis, William, 100

Deaver, Michael, 69, 72

Derwinski, Edward, 113

Diefenbaker, John, 38

Dingell, John, 51, 71–2

diplomacy
- new, in the United States, vii, 11, 117, 151; as lobbying, 26, 76; rules of, 27; as public activity, 37, 53; microstrategies and principles of, 53, 56–63; access as vital to, 63
- traditional, vii; rules of, 11–16; and domestic affairs, 14–15; under strain, 17

  See also ambassador

disputes, Canada–U.S., 18, 37; as public-policy conflicts, 45–7, 133–4; over ban on asbestos, 37, 50–1; over countervail action of Ontario corn producers, 61–2; over drug regulations, 51–2; over lobster fishing, 52–3; over processed pork, 37, 62–3; over trucking regulation, 48–50, 142–3. *See also* acid rain, Arctic sovereignty, border broadcasting, dispute settlement, East Coast fishery, International Joint Commission

dispute settlement, third-party (Canada–U.S.): as augmenting methods of new diplomacy, 117, 148–9; traditional Canadian resistance to, 135–8; Canadian experience with, 136–8; bilateral (Canada–U.S.) institutions used as mechanisms for, 140–7, 150. *See also* International Joint Commission

Dodd, Christopher, 80

Domenici, Peter, 59

Durenburger, David, 61, 106, 131

Dymond, Bill, 111

Eagleburger, Lawrence, 97
East Coast fishery, proposed agreement on, 18–21, 39, 45, 69,
    143–4
Eisenhower, Dwight, 85
Enders, Thomas, 55, 97
Evans, Rowland, 6
External Affairs, Department of: role of in management of
    foreign affairs, 120–4. *See also* multiplicity-of-instruments
    doctrine

free-trade agreement, Canada and United States. *See* Canada–U.S.
    Free Trade Agreement
Fried, Jonathan, 111

Galbraith, John Kenneth, 77
Georges Bank. *See* East Coast fishery
Gibbons, Sam, 89, 109–10
Goldwater, Barry, 57, 60
Gorsuch, Ann, 68
government, United States: main features of, 27–9, 43–4;
    executive-branch role in, 44, 53 (*see also* president)

Haig, Alexander, 96, 141
Hart, Gary, 40
Heinz, John, 56, 57, 66,
Henderson, Sir Nicholas, 34
Holmes, John, 139

International Joint Commission (IJC): establishment of, 138; role
    of in settling Canada–U.S. boundary-water disputes, 134–5
Johnson, Lyndon B., 30, 85
Judd, Jim, 61

Keating Five, 40, 82
Kennedy, Edward, 20
Kennedy, John F., 38, 40, 85
King, William Lyon Mackenzie, 94

lawyers, in Washington, 32, 90
Laxalt, Paul, 80
Legault, Leonard, 111
Lewis, Drew, 100
lobbyists, in Washington, 31–3, 59–60, 89–90; foreign, 32, 44, 71,
    76; trade associations as, 32, 90
lobsters. *See* disputes
Long, Russell, 107
Lougheed, Peter, 127
Lugar, Richard, 80
Lukens, Charles, 67–8

MacEachen, Allan, 140–1
McFarlane, Robert, 69, 104
MacGuigan, Mark, 96, 140–1
Matsunaga, Spark, 106–7
Meese, Edwin, 85
Mitchell, George, 53, 57, 73
Mondale, Walter, 85
Moynihan, Patrick Daniel, 36, 55, 56, 57, 66, 105
Mulroney, Brian, 68–9, 74, 98–9, 102, 114–15, 128, 141
multiplicity-of-instruments doctrine: as augmenting methods of
    new diplomacy, 117, 151; defined and contrasted with tradi-
    tional Canadian approach to relations with United States,
    117–18, 125–7; as currently realized in Canada–U.S. functional
    contacts, 119–20; hazards of, 127–9; role of Canadian Embassy
    under, 129–30; as extension of lobbying process, 131–2

Nielsen, Erik, 128

O'Neill, Tip, 29

Packwood, Robert, 58, 106
Palmerston, Henry, Lord, 57
Pearson, Lester, 139
Pell, Claiborne, 19, 20–2, 23–5, 55
Peterson, David, 106, 131

159

Pitfield, Michael, 123

political-action committees (PACs), 33, 77

Porter, William, 121

Powell, Colin, 114

power, political, in Washington, 31–2. *See also* Congress, lobbyists, president, special interests

presidency, 'imperial,' 10, 79–80

president of United States: as chairman of the board, 84–5; and chief of staff, 85; and conduct of foreign affairs, 17–18, 22-3, 80, 95; powers and image of, contrasted with Congress, 81–2, 83; role of in Arctic sovereignty dispute, 114–15; role of in trade disputes, 73, 75–6, 80; and vice-president, 85

Randolph, Jennings, 64–5

Rayburn, Sam, 30

Reagan, Ronald, 8, 14, 23, 38, 68–9, 70, 74, 75, 80, 84, 85, 96–7, 99–100, 102, 107, 114–15, 141

Regan, Donald, 85, 104

Reisman, Simon, 108

Robinson, Paul, 68

Roosevelt, Franklin D., 94

Roosevelt, Theodore, 137

Rudman, Warren, 52

separation of powers, doctrine of, 17, 27, 43

Shultz, George, 67, 69, 91, 112, 140–1

Simpson, Alan, 87

Skelton, O.D., 123

Solarz, Stephen, 80

special-interest groups, in Washington, 35, 43, 47, 76, 77, 88; foreign governments as, 44, 76, 78. *See also* Congress, lobbyists

Stafford, Robert, 58–9

State Department, U.S., role of in trade negotiations, 91–2

Strauss, Robert, 29, 98

sub-separation of powers, doctrine of, 27–8, 29, 43. *See also* Congress

Sununu, John, 67, 86

Thatcher, Margaret, 98
Thordardson, Janice, 65
Tower, John, 40
trucking. *See* disputes
Trudeau, Pierre Elliott, 8, 18, 23, 38, 96, 97, 98, 123, 143

Vance, Cyrus, 19

Warner, John, 59
Wilson, Michael, 111
Wright, Jim, 40, 77, 82

Zorinski, Edward, 62–3